Foundational Networking™

Building Know, Like and Trust
To Create A Lifetime of Extraordinary Success

Frank Agin

Foundational Networking™

Building Know, Like and Trust
To Create A Lifetime of Extraordinary Success

Frank Agin

Printed in the United States of America

Permission in the United States of America

Permission to reproduce or transmit in any form or by any means, electronic or mechanical, including photocopying and recording, or by an information storage and retrieval system, must be obtained by writing to the author, Frank Agin. He may be contacted at the following address:

Am*Spirit*™
BUSINESS *CONNECTIONS*
Post Office Box 30724, Columbus, Ohio 43230
Toll free: (888) 267-7474 • Email: frankagin@amspirit.com

Ordering Information:
To order additional copies, contact your local bookstore.
Quantity discounts are available.

ISBN: 978-0-9823332-1-1

Published by:

418
PRESS
A Division of Four Eighteen Enterprises LLC
Post Office Box 30724
Columbus, Ohio 43230-0724

Copy editing: Sherrie Bossart
Proofreading: David Smith,
Frances Jackson & Michael Agin
Cover and Interior design:
Rick Shaffer, rshaffer@shafferdesign.com,
Shaffer Design Works, LLC

Dedication

Lucas, Logan & Chase
Never Forget ... Your Greatest Day Is Yet To Come.

Author's Notes and Acknowledgements

Being involved with, managing or owning AmSpirit Business Connections for close to 15 years, I have had more than an average exposure to material on the subject of professional networking. I have read countless books and articles … attended numerous presentations and programs … and received more than my share of unsolicited advice.

Each of these publications, presentations and insightful monologues has had some value. Each provided a litany of skills and techniques that served to make me (or anyone who witnessed them) more successful through professional networking – where to go, when to speak and what to say. While all of this material offered value, it was missing something.

At first, I could not identify what that something was. It was merely a hunch. This intuition came from the fact that I saw people employing these skills and techniques every day, and yet many of these people were getting very little, if anything, from their networking efforts.

Then in 2005, I enrolled in a program through Leadership Management, Inc. (LMI) on organizational and personal leadership. Michael Diercks, the lead instructor, devoted almost the entire first session to talking about skills and techniques (the actual terms he used were "skills and knowledge") versus attitudes and habits. He explained that skills and techniques allow us to start our own businesses or are what convince people to hire us. It is, however, our attitudes and habits that determine whether we are successful.

At that moment, I understood what was missing from all the material on professional networking. Moreover, at that moment I understood why some people were so great with networking skills and techniques, but struggled to derive anything of value from their networking. What drives our success in professional networking (or anything else for that matter) is our attitudes and habits. From that one epiphany, the notion for this book, *Foundational Networking*, was born.

Of all the people I want to thank, my wife, Linda, and three children (Lucas, Logan and Chase) come first. Certainly, any moment spent on researching, writing and editing this book was time away from them and my obligations as a husband and father.

In addition, I want to thank Rick Shaffer for his design work. I also want to thank Ron Finklestein for connecting me to him … and Laura Leggett for introducing me to Ron … and Jeff Houck for introducing me to Laura … and Reagan Rodriguez for introducing me to Jeff … and Michael Diercks for introducing me to Reagan. This certainly underscores the notion that we accomplish nothing alone.

I certainly want to thank Michael Diercks with LMI. Not only did Mike provide the ignition to get this project moving (and in a round about way connect me with Morgan James Publishing), he consulted with me on a weekly basis over 18 long months as I wrote and re-wrote various sections of *Foundational Networking*.

In addition to Michael Diercks, I appreciate the input and insight from those six others I had been meeting with every Monday morning at the AmSpirit Business Connections Development Forum – Tom Anderson, Jim Coe, Jared Cummins, David Gamble, George Schulz and David Smith. Whether they realize it or not, our weekly interactions were important to the development of *Foundational Networking*.

There is also the AmSpirit Business Connections leadership team, whose efforts kept the organization moving along as I devoted time and energy to drafting this tome. These include Tom Anderson (Excelleweb), Julie Barhorst (Horizon Payroll Services), Dean Curry (Curry & Associates), Michael Diercks (Leadership Management Institute), Neal Gray (The Anderson Gray Group), Sheri Gunn (Open Sky Bodyworks), Jeff Houck (Surfside Business Concepts), Earl Phillips (Phillips Design), Reagan Rodriguez (Franchise Business Advisors), Terri Schulze (Pure Water), Dave Smith (Performance Dynamics) and Gina Weisenbarger (Panagea Networks).

As with anything of this magnitude, there are many people who lent support.

There is my personal editor, Sherrie Bossart. There is AmSpirit Business Connections' Marketing Assistant, Amber Flack. There is John Millen with Mainstream Leadership Communication, who helped me frame the direction of the book. There is Michael Perez with Ameriprise Financial and Toastmaster District 40 Governor, who reviewed my manuscript and offered commentary. And there are countless other people who provided me with ideas, insights and thoughts.

Finally, I need to thank the literally hundreds of entrepreneurs, sales representatives and professionals who are part of the membership of AmSpirit Business Connections. All of them are my clients. They have provided me a unique opportunity to serve them and at the same time allowed me to learn through their experiences. Most of them are my avid supporters. Business ownership is a challenge, and they have spurred me on when I needed it most. Many of them are my friends. What a wonderful thing to have so many positive people with whom to associate.

In closing, I intend what follows in this book to be the guiding philosophy for myself and AmSpirit Business Connections. Always remember, "Become the person you want to network with."

Frank Agin
February 26, 2008

Endorsements

Frank Agin's point is clear: It is not what you know, and it is not necessarily who you know. It is all about how you interact with them.
— Michelle Adams, President, Prism Marketing Communications

Anyone who has read any of my books or articles knows that my ongoing themes are building one-on-one relationships, creating trust and credibility with everyone you touch, and serving others through the mantra of 'What goes around, comes around'. Frank Agin's book, Foundational Networking, beautifully, simply and effectively addresses all three through his concepts of presence, altruism and integrity in order to help you become the kind of person with whom you yourself would like to associate.
— Dr. Tony Alessandra, Author, The Platinum Rule and Charisma

Foundational Networking has a unique approach … Frank's insights makes it easy to build real, lasting relationships in business and life.
— Steve Baldzicki, President & Founder, Big Fish Networking

Insightful and motivating. Frank has a keen understanding of the human spirit.
— Peg Buckley, CPA, The MP Group, LLP

Foundational Networking provides more than an basis for critical thinking on how to be successful at forming and maintaining business relationships. It is also an excellent motivational guide to your everyday life. It provides a useful toolbox in developing techniques to improve your interpersonal skills.
— Frank Carrino, General Counsel, Westfield Insurance Group

Read this book! It will help you implement strategies to take both your personal and professional relationships to a new level of performance.
— Ron Finklestein, Author, 49 Marketing Secrets (THAT WORK) to Grow Sales & The Platinum Rule for Small Business Mastery

Foundational Networking clearly spells it out … networking success — as with anything – is all about attitude.
— Rick Frishman, Co-Author, Where's Your Wow

Frank goes beyond the usual networking advice to show how taking blame, saying you're sorry, and forgiving others can help build the foundation to success. His emphasis on ethics truly inspires business people to aim higher.
— Jeff Grabmeier, Director of Research Communications The Ohio State University

Networking for a small business starting out is the great equalizer. This book gets it!
  — Barney Greenbaum, President, FranNet, Central & Southeastern Ohio

Frank captures very insightful and true concepts that he has learned through his own personal development and experiences. He brings an upbeat and positive message to networking that will work for you. Frank's networking message relates to a better way of being, a higher calling for all of us who think of ourselves as business people.
  — Jim Hatch, Director of Seminars, Virginia Continuing Legal Education

Frank Agin's wonderful work can be captured in a single word 'influence.' Where there is influence there is power. Where there is power there is a network. Why would any of us settle for anything less?
  — Harvey Hook, Author, The Power of an Ordinary Life

In this book, you will understand why Frank Agin's foundational principles are necessary in building lasting, productive relationships that create mind-blowing success!
  — Lewis Howes, Founder, SportsNetworker.com
  Co-Author, LinkedWorking

I wish this book had been around when I first started networking more than 20 years ago. It is a step-by-step guide on how to create powerful, lasting relationships.
  — Christine Kinney, CEG
  Mom Coach & Cofounder of Like Minded Moms Networking Group

Foundational Networking offers innovative thinking on how those wishing to build their network can do so through building relationships. This book is a great tool for building your networking foundation."
  — Lisa K. Kunkle, Vice President, General Counsel and Secretary
  PolyOne Corporation

Frank has captured the essence of "networking" in this book. It is philosophical – yet very practical.
  — David Leopold, Author
  How Do You Answer These 749 Questions About Your Small Business?

Foundational Networking establishes Frank Agin as America's leading expert on building real, not superficial, relationships through networking.
  — John Millen, President, Mainstream Leadership Communication

This should be the first networking book you read. It will become the manual for networking development for the 21st century.
– Lee Rankinen, Assistant Football Coach, Maine Maritime Academy

An excellent resource for anyone who wants to build a strong network that keeps on working.
– Reagan Rodriguez, CEO, Franchise Business Advisors

Finally, a straight-forward investigation covering the most important aspects of successful networking, and living life.
– Tim Stauffer, President, SideHire.com

Frank Agin's practical and inspiring insights on what leads to success in business relationships is based on years of "in the trenches" experience. In this book, he shares his best tips, which are sure to produce positive results for every reader.
– Barbara Wayman, APR, President, BlueTree Media, LLC

This book is truly a foundation or philosophy of networking. Frank is adding so much to the concept of networking. This book will give you the framework to build and understand the importance of networking in any career.
– Dr. Keith Winfree, President, CEO and Founder
Winfree Business Growth Advisors

Contents

Introducing Foundational Networking

> "With the furious pace of change in business today, difficulty to manage relationships sabotages more business than anything else – it is not a question of strategy that gets us in trouble, it's a question of emotions."
> — *John Kotter*

This book will change the way you think about networking. More importantly, once you adopt and embrace this change in thinking, this book will have a profound effect on your actual networking. You will find that you are getting dramatically more from your network. In addition, you will discover that what you generate from your network will require that you expend a whole lot less effort. Finally, you will realize just how enjoyable and fulfilling networking can be.

While this is a book about networking, it is not a book about networking skills. In this book, you will come to the understanding that the networking skills you have worked to hone and perfect are limited in their ability to serve you.

This limitation does not mean that you need to develop more networking skills, different networking skills or even better networking skills. The networking skills you have are more than adequate. This limitation, rather, is simply a function of the fact that your skills in networking (or anything) can only do so much for you. What is important, however, are your attitudes and habits toward the people around you, yourself and your situation in life (past, present and future). It is these attitudes and habits that serve as a base upon which your networking skills operate.

This is a book about what I call "foundational networking." Foundational networking is the process of building the "know, like and trust" in your network. Foundational networking allows you to make the most of the networking skill you have. Furthermore, it will allow you to get more out of new networking skills you will develop.

The underlying theme of foundational networking is simply this: to reach your potential at networking you need to *endeavor to become that person with whom you would like to associate*. We all have an image in our mind of the types of people we would like to connect with. When you start acting in a manner consistent with that image, that is exactly the type of people you will attract. Moreover, by becoming that person, you have transformed yourself into a person that other people desire to get to know (as they likely have conjured up a similar image).

Discovery Of Foundational Networking

While this book is about attitudes and habits, it is nevertheless about networking. This is a book about finding lasting success through networking by adopting a new mindset toward yourself and others (attitudes) and then allowing that new thought pattern to manifest itself in your everyday actions (habits). Given that premise, you may ask what qualifies me to address the subject matter. The answer to that is quite simple: life.

For substantially more time than I have done anything else I have worked to help small business America become more successful through networking. As founder and president of AmSpirit Business Connections, I am someone who has built a business laboring in the networking trenches. My days are spent educating and empowering entrepreneurs, sales representatives and professionals to become more successful by establishing and developing productive business relationships.

On the networking front, I have worked directly with hundreds of small business types in almost every imaginable line of business, which would include (just to scratch the surface) attorneys, accountants, mortgage lenders, financial advisors, realtors, insurance agents and bankers. In addition, I have worked with people at various levels of corporate America, including those who experienced downsizing and job elimination. Finally, I have trained and empowered dozens of people who are involved in AmSpirit Business Connections as either area directors or franchisees.

On a daily basis, I have had a firsthand view of what works and what does not in relation to networking. Additionally, I hear about many networking successes and failures.

Through this experience, I have seen and heard of people with great networking skills who are completely frustrated because their networking efforts appear to be returning fewer benefits than they are expecting. At the same time, I see and hear of people with, at best, marginal skills experiencing phenomenal networking results.

While these observations were perplexing to me initially, I made a closer examination into this seemingly inconsistent situation. Through examining research and reading books on human interaction, business relations and group dynamics as well as participating in programs on similar topics, it became clear to me what was occurring. Quite simply, people's networking skills were a whole lot less important than their attitudes and habits toward themselves and the people around them.

It was not surprising to me then when I found that this conclusion clearly manifested itself in each of the situations I observed. As I got to know the people involved better and had conversations with those who knew these individuals, without exception the answers all related back to foundational networking.

The people with great skills and frustrating results had some sort of deficiency relative to their foundational networking. Somehow or another it turned out they had a poor attitude toward either themselves or the people around them and this was carrying over into their habits for interacting with others. The greatest of networking skills could not compensate for the fact that few people knew them, liked them or trusted them.

Alternatively, there are the "marginal skills" people who enjoyed incredible results simply because of superior foundational networking. While their networking skills may have been lacking, they more than overcame this deficiency by the mere fact that a great many people knew them, liked them and trusted them. Quite frankly, their marginal networking skills had minimal impact on their networking results.

I freely acknowledge that the skills are important. I have, however, learned from research, reading and study that foundational networking does exist. More importantly, I have found from first hand observations that foundational networking is far more imperative to success than all of the networking skills you could ever learn.

Foundational Networking Clarified

Do you want to be successful? As you are reading this book, the answer is obvious. No matter how you choose to define it, you want more out of life than you already have – personally and professionally. As a result, you work hard to achieve greater success.

As part of this drive, you engage in various networking activities – attending business functions, joining organizations and connecting one-on-one with whomever you can. To aid you in this process, you have no doubt obtained knowledge from the plethora of books, tapes and seminars that exist on the subject. In addition, you have likely consulted with others in an effort to be more effective at networking.

These materials and conversations with others provided you knowledge on the skills necessary to work a room, construct a short personal commercial for yourself and manage a handful of accumulated business cards. They offered insight into the skills necessary to meet new people, carry a conversation and then follow up after the fact. These teachings suggested an endless list of other skills that you assumed would serve to surround you with a legion of others who could not help but raise you to new heights.

Skills are important. Without solid skills, your success in networking will not reach its potential. Skills alone are not enough, however. To have truly great networking success you need to combine your networking skills with certain other intangible attributes – attitudes and habits focused on building "know, like and trust."

As for the various materials available on networking success, the authors certainly mention the importance of know, like and trust. They fail to address how to build it, though. Generally, the discussion in the vast majority of this material is only a passing mention – such as "To be successful in networking, it is important that people know, like and trust you."

Whether or not these authors are aware of the attitudes and habits that build know, like and trust is unclear. What is clear is that anything related to what I term foundational networking is beyond the scope of their material. Their primary aim is to devote their material to networking skills, as if there is nothing more.

However, there is more. There is so much more. While skills are important to networking success, these attitudes and habits that build know, like and trust are vital. Simply stated, if people do not know you, like you and trust you, then it does not matter how adept you are with respect to your networking skills. Without a solid base of know, like and trust built by these attitudes and habits, your networking skills will fail you every time.

Compare this to the concept of a house. A house has two basic aspects. The first is everything above the ground. This would include the floor, the walls, the roof, the windows, the doors and everything else you can see. These are all important aspects of any house. Without these, you do not have much of a shelter.

The second basic aspect is the foundation. It is the combination of concrete and cement blocks that the contractor builds below the ground. The first thing that any contractor establishes when building a house is the foundation. Nothing else can happen until the contractor gets this done.

On top of the foundation, a contractor will place a floor and upon the floor, the contractor will set walls. On the walls, the contractor will then attach doors and windows. Then, on top of the walls, the contractor will place the roof. Following this proven building sequence, a house will last for decades, if not hundreds of years.

You can build a house without a foundation. But without the foundation, the house will last only a few short years, if that long. Without a firmly anchored foundation, the floor will shift. Once the floor shifts, the walls move to compensate. When the walls move, windows break and doors become jammed open or stuck shut. Once the walls have moved, the roof loses all support and no longer has structural integrity.

Yes, everything above the ground is important to make the house a livable shelter. The foundation, however, is imperative to the long-term viability of a house.

Your true networking potential is much like a house. Your networking skills are analogous to everything above the ground. Just as a house will not last without a strong foundation, your networking skills alone – no matter how proficient – will not ensure networking success.

To reach your true networking potential, you need to set your skills upon a solid foundation. This foundation is being "known, liked and trusted." Without this foundation, as with a house, even the most perfected networking skills will not result in effective networking.

Again, foundational networking is the process of building the know, like and trust in your network and you do it whenever you focus on certain attitudes and habits. This is not to say that networking skills are of no value and that there is no merit in developing them. Networking skills are important. All other things being equal, someone with exemplary networking skills will always realize far better results than someone with average skills.

However, not all things are equal. There are those who are well known, greatly liked and implicitly trusted. Alternatively, there are those who are little known, generally disliked and simply not trusted. Moreover, lots of others are at various places somewhere in between. Networking success will always favor those with a higher degree of being known, liked and trusted regardless of proficiency of networking skills.

This book will be devoted entirely to exploring the attitudes and habits you need to develop to build know, like and trust, which is your strong networking foundation. Equally important, this book will discuss ways in which we can harness foundational networking so you can continually enhance the knowing, liking and trusting that others have in you.

The Component Parts Of Foundational Networking

Foundational networking hinges on adopting the attitudes and habits so that others know, like and trust you. However, this begs the question: What is know, like and trust? Certainly, we can come up with an almost too apparent description for each:

- **Know:** Others gaining an understanding of who you are based on how you conduct yourself generally.

- **Like:** Others having a strong favorable feeling toward you based on how you contribute generally to the world around you.

- **Trust:** Others perceiving you as being reliable, honest and trustworthy based on their personal interactions with you (or their personal observations of your interactions with others).

However, these terms and their respective descriptions are an indication of the end result and do nothing to address how you get there. For example, why do people want to know you and what do they want to know about you? What causes them to like you (or would cause them to dislike you)? How do you generate trust with others?

In working to build each of these foundational networking results – know, like and trust – there are many underlying traits and characteristics upon which to focus your attitudes and habits.

For example, pulling from the above definition of trust, it is evident that you develop trust through demonstrating reliability, honesty and trustworthiness. Therefore, through foundational networking you need to embark on a course to alter your attitudes and adopt habits that make you (or at least make you seem) more reliable, honest and trustworthy.

For foundational networking, all these traits and characteristics can be broken down into three basic categories or components: presence, altruism and integrity. Please understand, however, that these three basic categories of traits and characteristics are not limited to a strict dictionary definition. Rather, for illustrating what comprises foundational networking or building know, like and trust, I use these three terms in a general sense.

The presence component of foundational networking involves your attitudes and habits toward how you carry yourself and how you appear to others. In part, it involves your:

- Contentment with your life and your optimism for the future;
- Resiliency in overcoming or working through setbacks and adversity; and
- Courage to take on challenges and explore new experiences.

The *altruism* component of the foundational networking involves all your attitudes and habits related to your disposition toward contributing to the lives of others. In part, it involves your:

- Tendency to be generous with your resources, contacts and talents;
- Eagerness to show appreciation for those things that others have done for you;
- Propensity to have compassion for others and their situations; and
- Willingness to praise others for their achievements, compliment them for their desirable attributes and encourage them to press on.

Finally, the *integrity* component of foundational networking includes your attitudes and habits with respect to how you interact with others. In part, it involves your:

- Conviction to treat others fairly and honestly;
- Commitment to being unwaveringly dependable and reliable;
- Sincerity in recognizing your own faults;
- Willingness to apologize when your actions (or inactions) cause harm;
- Ability to share the praise and recognition with others; and,
- Willingness to accept the responsibility of your role in setbacks.

In summary, foundational networking is the process of building know, like and trust in your network. You do this whenever you focus on the attitudes and habits that serve to:

- Improve your *presence*;
- Enhance your *altruism*; and,
- Bolster your *integrity*.

In this book, I devote significant time to each of these components and their various underlying traits and characteristics. This book will give you a new way to think about your networking. In addition, it will provide you answers as to why your networking efforts are not as effective as you might hope them to be. Finally, this book will offer you ideas for improving the attitudes and habits you need to focus on in the course of foundational networking, which will help to better build the necessary know, like and trust with others in your network.

Foundational Networking Is Networking

Certainly, at this point in the book, some of you may be concluding that this is not a book about networking – rather this is simply a book about being a good citizen of the world. That is the point. Being a good citizen of the world, as manifested in our presence, altruism and integrity, is imperative to networking success.

No, this is not a book about networking skills. However, it is certainly a book about networking – networking from the perspective of building know, like and trust within your network. For this reason, what you will find in this book will have much more powerful and far-reaching consequences for you than any other networking book you have ever read or program you will ever attend.

Believe this: foundational networking is networking. Without a strong, stable networking foundation, your networking skills are limited in effectiveness at best and completely ineffective at worst.

Still others of you may conclude, "But I have a so-called foundation, so there is no value in me reading on." It is true. You do have a networking foundation. Everyone does to one degree or another. However, you are not perfect. Given that alone, you will benefit from continuing to read.

This book is about understanding the attitudes and habits you need to focus on in the course of foundational networking. In turn, this will help you better build the necessary know, like and trust with others in your network.

For these reasons, this book is definitely worth your while. After all, if you commit to embarking on a regimen of foundational networking, you will enjoy long-term networking success. If you combine your foundational networking with continued development of networking skills, the sky is the limit.

Presence

> "The most precious gift we can
> offer others is our presence."
> — *Thich Nhat Hanh*

From the moment you walk into any room, the foundational networking begins. You set about building the know, like and trust among those who are or will be in your network and generally this is before you have even spoken a word.

Everyone who sees you begins to evaluate you. In this informal assessment, they observe your demeanor, mannerisms and even body language. Within just a few short seconds, whether they know it or not, they all draw several conclusions about you. They conclude whether you are friendly or stoic. They decide whether you are open or aloof. They make these determinations and perhaps a dozen more.

In fact, now in the electronic age this can happen even before the point of meeting someone in person. How you answer the telephone creates an initial impression on others. Does your "hello" indicate "I am open to talking with you"? Or does your "hello" make them feel uneasy about continuing the call.

Even the manner in which you reply to e-mails can give others clues. While this form of assessment may be less reliable than a face-to-face encounter, it still gives others a way to evaluate you. From just a few short words, they are able to determine much about you. Are you exasperated or interested? Are you hurried or calm? Are you hospitable or standoffish?

These are first impressions. Like it or not, they serve as a preview of your attitudes and habits. In turn, these impressions determine whether you are building know, like and trust in your network.

This process, however, is not limited to your point of first contact. Beyond these initial impressions, people continue to draw conclusions about you through future interactions, whether in person, on the telephone or over the Internet. Their conclusions center on various clues, which include, but are hardly limited to, your facial expressions, posture and tone of voice.

In essence, they are making a determination as to whether or not you are someone with whom they would like to associate. For the most part, these individuals conduct this evaluation completely independent of the networking skills you demonstrate.

There is nothing wrong with this. In fact, if you think about it, you will admit that you do the same thing. You are continually making assessments and evaluations of others.

In fact, devote some time to visualizing someone with whom you would like to associate. Whether this is someone new or someone you already know, the person likely has a certain air about him.

This so-called air is a combination of characteristics or traits. You might describe it as a sort of moxie that seems to say in a quiet fashion, "bring on the day and I will ensure that good things will follow." You may call this optimism. Or you may call it determination. Or still you might refer to it as a sort of confidence. In simplest terms, this person has got "it," whatever it actually is.

Certainly, you do not envision a person who is continually down or moody. It is doubtful that you have images of the person who looks to others for inspiration and motivation. It is unlikely to be the person who sincerely believes that life or situations cannot get any better.

No, you want to surround yourself with those whose mere presence offers a sort of uplifting power. You cannot help but feel more optimistic, more determined and more confident when you are around them.

If this is the person with whom you envision associating, then endeavor to become that person. Work to develop that "it" – the moxie, confidence and determination that calls out to others.

Again, under the Law of Attraction, the person you become is the person you will attract. Furthermore, if you envision this person, it is likely that others do too. Therefore, by becoming this person, you become the object of their networking desire.

This sort of persona or personal swagger that you should adopt and maintain is the presence component of foundational networking. These are the qualities that serve to build your know, like and trust. Frankly, when you have this "it," others are more eager to know you, quicker to like you and will trust you that much more easily.

Mind you, this component has very little to do with what you say and almost everything to do with how you project certain qualities, some of which can include candor, passion and poise. In fact, more than 80 percent of what we communicate is non-verbal. For example, the Gettysburg Address ("Four score and seven years ago …"), given by a confident and resolved Abraham Lincoln, would not have had nearly the impact had he mumbled it with uncertainty and dispassion. It was how Lincoln delivered this message and not the message itself that made it so powerful.

However, the notion of enhancing your presence may be something that you have considered impossible. You may have surmised that either you had it or you did not. In any respect, there was no changing that.

Understand, however, that enhancing your presence is possible. The means of doing so may not be readily apparent. This is primarily because there is no clear definition or quantifiable standard of what you might have termed as "it." After all, your presence is not pegged to a particular hairstyle, being a certain height or wearing a definite style of clothes. No one can really define "it." Yet, you certainly know it when you see "it" or, better yet, know it when you do not.

Nevertheless, enhancing your presence is possible. It is simply a matter of working to adopt certain attitudes and focusing on creating certain habits. These attitudes and habits then project to others that you are someone with whom they want to associate.

It is important to note that developing a networking presence is similar to being healthy and physically fit. Becoming healthy and physically fit is not something you obtain and then always have, such as a Bachelor of Arts or Science or United States citizenship.

To maintain a strong cardiovascular system, you need to continually log time and miles in the pool, on your feet or on a bike. To sustain good muscle tone, you must periodically expose your muscles to some sort of resistance. To keep overall health, you need to moderate your intake of junk food and have the proverbial "apple a day" or other things of comparable nutritional value.

The same holds true for presence – getting it takes tremendous effort and concentration. However, keeping it takes the same. Your presence is established or squandered on an almost continual basis.

Thus, you cannot believe or assume that because at one point you have presence, that you will always have it. There are times when you have it and others when you do not. Whether or not you have it is a function of attitudes and habits that serve to build the degree to which others know, like and trust you.

What are the attitudes and habits of presence as it relates to foundational networking? This entire section is devoted to exploring this question.

None of these attitudes and habits is overly complicated in nature. Furthermore, most of these attitudes and habits are relatively easy for you to adopt or implement. In fact, you may exhibit many of them from time to time.

While you may exhibit them, they may or may not be routine. Even if you have made any, some or all routine, you likely do not equate them to your overall networking success (or lack thereof). This is the essence of foundational networking – our presence is an imperative element to our success in building know, like and trust.

Sense of Humor

"Humor is the great thing, the saving thing.
The minute it crops up, all our irritations
and resentments slip away and a
sunny spirit takes their place."
— Mark Twain

Having a good sense of humor – whether you are creating the laughter or simply enjoying it – is essential to getting people to know, like and trust you.

Ask yourself, who are you drawn to, someone who expresses his or her sense of humor on a consistent basis or the person who makes every moment ultra-serious? Of course, these are two extremes. Nevertheless, if you had to lean one way or another, which would it be? If you consider this question carefully, you would probably conclude that you would be much more comfortable associating with the person with a sense of humor.

Laughter, which is the productive result of humor, is the universal language. It is something that every culture enjoys – there has never been (and likely never will be) a society that does not embrace a good chuckle. It is something that people of all ages take pleasure in – from tiny babies to those on their deathbeds. It transcends economic status – the rich, the poor, and everyone in between enjoy a good laugh (although maybe not at the same things).

The enjoyment of laughter is one quality that you have in common with everyone on the planet. As such, it would make sense that, all things being equal, you would opt to associate with the individual who demonstrates a good sense of humor over someone who does not.

I realize that you may have heard or read a statement like, "There is no place in business for humor." I know I have.

Whenever I hear or read a statement like this, I imagine the person uttering this is doing so in a very low, deep, booming voice. Immediately, I feel like I am a kid again at Aunt Millie's house on Easter Sunday. Everything is prim and proper and the only thing Mom and Dad will allow me to do – for fear of inadvertently tampering with a lace doily – is watch television ... black and white ... either CBS or PBS.

Unfortunately, far too often we buy into it. Think about it. You are one person at home – fun loving, with a wide-ranging sense of humor. Then everyone expects you to be someone else when the workday begins – stoic and ever serious.

Much is wrong with this mindset. Certainly, this attitude strips a degree of enjoyment out of what amounts to the lion's share of our day. More importantly, this is not a good practice of foundational networking.

Yes, there is the risk that humor will serve to tarnish your image of being mature and professional. Additionally, there is humor that is simply not in good taste. Thus, in today's politically correct environment you need to be careful with when and how you employ humor. This does not mean that we need to abandon it altogether, however.

Certainly, this is not advocating that you develop an arsenal of jokes that center on religious figures and societal ills, such as prostitution. Nor is this advocating that you make insulting commentary regarding the shortcomings of others. Moreover, this is not to say that you need to be a stand-up comedy type with witty comebacks and rib-splitting one-liners.

The point is that you should not avoid humor. You do not need a stage or everyone's focus to direct attention to an ironic situation (such as a boss who clamors for more productivity but cannot help but take a mid-afternoon nap).

You can also ease the stress of a generally tension-filled business environment by simply throwing out an off-handed comment. These humoristic remarks need only generate a mere smile and a chuckle. It can be nothing more than a comment about the weather, the local favorite sports team or the quality of office coffee.

On the other hand, to enhance your foundational networking presence you do not necessarily need to be the source of the levity. You can add to the lightness of the moment by laughing at the humor of others or acknowledging them for their wit and comic relief.

Humor and laughter remind others that you are human. It is something with which anyone can identify and it is something to which everyone is drawn. As long as it is appropriately used, it will make people more comfortable around you and thus more likely to associate with you.

In short, humor helps you build know, like and trust. It is nearly impossible to dislike someone who has made us laugh or is genuinely laughing at something funny. As a result, in the process of foundational networking, it is important that you must adopt the attitude that you are open to humor in your life and make a habit of finding it every day.

Foundational Networking Extra
A Funny Lesson From The Gipper

If you think that humor should be reserved for collegiate sophomoric behavior or for gathering of our closest friends and family, consider the late President Ronald Reagan, known for his portrayal of George "The Gipper" Gipp in the 1940s film "Knute Rockne – All American." Love or hate his politics, Reagan understood the importance of humor in advancing his agenda, taking on the opposition and connecting with the citizens of the United States.

In 1968, Richard Nixon had won the Republican nomination to run for President of the United States. Shortly thereafter, there was speculation that Nixon would select Reagan as his vice presidential running mate, to which Reagan replied, "There is absolutely no circumstance whatsoever under which I would accept that spot. Even if they tied and gagged me, I would find a way to signal by wiggling my ears."

In 1981, during an appearance at a Washington hotel, in a failed assassination attempt, a mentally ill John Hinkley, Jr. shot Reagan. With a bullet lodged just inches from his heart, Reagan handled the crisis with his trademark wit and self-assurance. Upon meeting the doctor who was to remove the bullet, Reagan is said to have quipped, "I hope you're a Republican."

In 1984, Reagan was 73 and running for re-election against a much younger Walter Mondale. While many on the Democratic side questioned whether he was too old to serve as President of the United States, Reagan remarked in a televised presidential debate, "I want you to know that I will not make age an issue of this campaign … I am not going to exploit, for political purposes, my opponent's youth and inexperience."

These are just a few of the dozens of humoristic remarks and actions of Ronald Reagan. He knew, and we should know, humor does not separate us from others. Rather, in reality, it draws us closer. Humor reminds others that we are human.

Reagan once jokingly remarked about why he liked to have a jar of jellybeans on hand for important meetings, "You can tell a lot about a fella's character by whether he picks out all of one color or just grabs a handful."

Reagan also taught us that you can tell a lot about someone's character by his sense of humor.

High Expectations

"Show me a thoroughly satisfied person,
and I will show you a failure."
— Thomas Edison

What is the expectation you have for yourself? What do you envision as the result of your determination and hard work? Alternatively, what do you see as the crowning achievement of your life?

Wherever your goals and aspirations have you pointed, you need to develop the mindset or expectation that your greatest day is yet to come. That is, you always need to be looking for more in your life – personally and professionally. This is a simple belief that no matter where you are in life – struggling to earn that last degree or certification or looking to step up one more rung on the corporate ladder – that a better day awaits you.

Continually envisioning this day keeps you motivated and striving for more. In addition, it justifies your hard work and determination. More importantly, the thought process that "there is always something greater for you" is a powerful attitude for foundational networking. People will want to know, like and trust you more if you have a high personal expectation and continual belief that your greatest day is yet to come.

Having this mentality of high personal expectation is not simply moving through life telling others that everything is "awesome." Rather, this underlying state of mind is an unspoken optimism with a blend of determination and confidence. It involves keeping yourself motivated, confident and believing.

This internal belief then carries over into how you conduct yourself. Your high personal expectation becomes like an aura that intrigues others to want to associate with you. From here, they want to become part of your network (no matter your level of networking skills).

Ask yourself this, with whom do you want to associate – the person whose crowning achievement is somewhere in the past or the person who is building toward a wonderful and monumental day? All things being equal, you want to associate with the person working toward and expecting to achieve something wonderful as opposed to someone whose greatest day is knowingly behind them. Therefore, become that person with a high personal expectation.

A useful analogy to underscore that point is the stock market. What does any reasonable investor look for – a company whose stock is trading at an all-time high relative to its history and the industry or the company with the stock price that presents tremendous opportunity? The investor looks for the stock with potential, as there is no value in what was.

Applying this same logic to personal relationships, the potential of the future excites people. They will want to associate themselves with you when you demonstrate an attitude of high personal expectation. They simply want to tap into the potential future value that this confidence represents.

In an effort to make this attitude a real part of your life, set about adopting these habits:

Personal Mission Statement: Develop a personal mission statement that you review on a periodic basis. In short, what is the underlying theme of your life? An example might be "To lead a long, healthy life marked by diverse personal and professional achievement as well as selfless contribution to others."

Goals: Establish specific, realistic goals for yourself that are in line with your personal mission statement. To be most effective, review these goals no less than weekly and write them out almost daily.

Visualization & Affirmation: Take time every day to affirm to yourself that you will achieve your goals and fulfill your mission. Then visualize yourself having achieved each, allowing you to experience the feeling of success in advance of getting there.

Self-Development: Commit to a program of ongoing self-development by continually finding relevant material to help you learn and grow. This can occur through reading, listening to audio programs or enrolling in programs that will benefit you.

Motivation: Seek out the people, situations and material that serve to motivate you and keep you striving for more and more.

As you practice each of these habits, never stop believing your greatest day is yet to come! If you do, you cannot help but have others who want to know, like and trust you.

Foundational Networking Exercise

What is your personal mission statement?

_____

_____

_____

_____

What are your specific, realistic goals? Where can you write them so you encounter them daily?

_____

_____

_____

When do you take time to visualize and affirm these goals?

_____

What are programs of self-development you are committed to engaging in?

_____

_____

_____

_____

Who are the people (or what are the situations and materials) that serve as a motivation to you?

_____

_____

Foundational Networking Extra

The Galatea Effect

In her book (as well as her July 25, 1986 *Kingsport Times-News* article) titled *Beliefs* Can *Influence Attitudes*, Nell Mohney shares a story of an experiment that was performed in a school in the San Francisco Bay area. With the assistance of Robert Rosenthal, a Harvard psychologist, school principal Lenore Jacobson called in three teachers and said, "Because you three teachers are the finest in the system and you have the greatest expertise, we're going to give you ninety selected high-IQ students. We're going to let you move these students through this next year at their pace and see how much they can learn."

The principal then met with the 90 students and their parents and gave them a similar message. In short, they were told that they were considered some of the brightest in the school system. As a result, they were each being assigned to one of three of the best teachers. With the assistance of their star instructor, they were encouraged to advance as far as they could over the course of the year.

Everyone – the three faculty members, the students, and the students' parents – thought this was a great idea. Who wouldn't? Anyone would love to be recognized as being outstanding. And besides, this was a special opportunity designed just for them. As anticipated, they all enjoyed the school year. By the time school ended, the students had achieved from 20 to 30 percent more than the other students in the entire San Francisco Bay area.

At the end of the year, the principal called in the three teachers and told them, "I have a confession to make. You did not have ninety of the most intellectually prominent students. They were run-of-the-mill students. We took ninety students at random from the system and gave them to you."

While feeling a bit confused, the teachers were proud of their achievement. They naturally concluded that their exceptional teaching skills must have been responsible for the students' great progress. This feeling of pride did not last, however.

"I have another confession," said principal Jacobson. "You're not the brightest of teachers. Your names were the first three drawn out of a hat."

Students whose names were drawn at random achieved extraordinarily above-average results while being taught by just any old teacher. How, then, did the students and teachers perform at such an exceptional level for an entire year? The answer can be found in their attitudes. They had an attitude of positive expectation – the teachers and students believed in themselves and one another. They performed well because they expected that they would.

People will go to great lengths to live up to the expectations that others have for them. Psychologists refer to this as the *Pygmalion Effect*, which comes from a story by Ovid about Pygmalion, a sculptor and prince of Cyprus.

Pygmalion created an ivory statue of his ideal woman, which he called Galatea. The figure was so beautiful that he immediately fell in love with it. Hence, Pygmalion begged the goddess Aphrodite to breathe life into the statue and make her his own. Aphrodite granted Pygmalion his wish, the statue came to life and the couple married and lived happily ever after.

The implication of the *Pygmalion Effect* for you is that what you get from the people in your network is no more or less than what you expect – so expect the best.

Similar to the *Pygmalion Effect* is the *Galatea Effect*. The Galatea Effect occurs when we create high expectations for ourselves. These high personal expectations in turn create greater personal achievement. That is, we act as our own Pygmalion, fulfilling our own prophecy about ourselves.

Contagiously Energetic

*"The simplest person, fired with enthusiasm,
is more persuasive than the most
eloquent person without it."*
— Franklin Field

There is little question, you are attracted to situations and individuals that create high energy. These people inspire your enthusiasm. As a result, you work harder for them. You are more attentive to their missions. Their energy seems to infect you.

You are not alone. Many others are attracted to these contagiously energetic people. Remarkably, the people who are attracted to these individuals are others with a similar attitude. This fact further inspires you. You definitely want to include this sort of person in your network.

Certainly, you are not attracted to situations and individuals that create a de-energizing environment. These people put a damper on your spirits and everyone else around them. While you might work for them, you dread doing so. You have no interest in advancing their cause.

In fact, rather than being attracted to them, you tend to avoid them. Whether you are successful in doing so, their mere presence is simply disheartening. Even if you can avoid them, you tend to waste time dreading the next encounter with them. You might even go so far as to mentally rehearse how you will cope. You do not want them to be part of your network.

Realizing this, you clearly want to adopt the attitudes and develop the habits that cast you as contagiously energetic. If you do this, people certainly will be attracted to you. They will want to get to know you. They will not be able to help but like you and they will make every effort to trust you.

To be an energizer, however, you must understand how to create energy, as it does not create itself. Then, you must commit to including this as part of your foundational networking strategy.

In their book, *The Hidden Power of Social Networks: Understanding How Work Really Gets Done in Organizations*, authors Rob Cross and Andrew Parker devote a chapter to the topic of creating energy. The authors' research involved a diverse selection of organizations such as consulting firms, financial services organizations, technology companies, government agencies and petrochemical businesses. Through their research, they examined the potential reasons for differences in human energy.

In summary, why do some organizations have an enthusiasm to them and others are simply de-energized? Why is it exciting to associate with some organizations and others are simply painful to be around? What makes certain groups inspiring while other groups are insipid?

The authors defined energy as a type of positive affective arousal, which people can experience as emotion (a short response to specific events) or mood (a longer-lasting state that need not be a response to a specific event). Then through their research, they identified five common characteristics or dimensions in high-energy organizations that were not present in less energetic organizations.

- **Dimension 1** *(Vision)*: Organizations energize those associated with them when they not only create a compelling, realistic vision for themselves, but also share it with members of the organization; and,

- **Dimension 2** *(Contribution)*: Organizations energize their members when they ensure that everyone is reasonably involved in providing input that serves to lead to the fulfillment of the organization's vision; and,

- **Dimension 3** *(Involvement)*: Organizations energize their members when they involve them in the execution of strategy to achieve the vision; and,

- **Dimension 4** *(Trust)*: Organizations energize their members as they continually demonstrate to members that they are committed in word and deed to the overall vision, which confirms the members' belief that the vision is attainable; and,

- **Dimension 5** *(Progress)*: Organizations energize members by providing a legitimate and ongoing sense that the organization is progressing toward achievement of the vision.

Certainly, the authors intended their research findings to aid corporate America, the not-for-profit world and governmental agencies. While the authors did not necessarily contemplate nor intend that their conclusions could influence the lives of individuals outside of the organizational setting, they certainly can.

Although it may be informal in nature, your network has a structure to it. Your network is not necessarily an entity similar to the ones analyzed in this research. It is, nevertheless, a loosely held organization.

Moreover, at the center of your network organization is you. Much like a corporate CEO or government official, you are the primary influencer of your network. As such, there is no reason why you cannot use the five common dimensions of a high-energy organization identified by Cross and Parker to energize your network.

Foundational Networking Exercise

You need to apply the findings of Cross and Parker to yourself as the leader of the informal organization called "your network." Working with individuals or small groups within your network, address the following:

VISION: You must take the time to crystallize in your mind where you envision certain individuals in your network will be taking you (and equally important, where you will take them). Then, you need to take the time to communicate this, at least informally.

- For example, "I see our businesses (or careers) developing hand-in-hand. This is how I see that working …"

- What is your compelling, realistic vision for those particular individuals in your network? Alternatively stated, what do you see the members of your network doing for you and what do you see yourself doing for them?

_____

_____

_____

_____

CONTRIBUTION: Once you have created and shared a compelling vision, these others will be excited about making it happen. They will have thoughts about how to further the process. Not only do you need to listen and be open-minded, you need to encourage their input.

- For example, "Do you have any thoughts on how we can accelerate this?"

- Now that you have shared your vision with certain individuals, what are their potential thoughts and ideas on achieving this vision?

_____

_____

_____

_____

INVOLVEMENT: The fulfillment of your vision requires the involvement of others. Thus, you need to find a way to involve them.

- For example, "Based on what we have discussed, here are the things that I will do and here are some things you can contribute." Alternatively, simply ask, "How would you like to contribute to this?"

- Summarize your role in fulfilling your vision as well as the roles of those with whom you are working through this.

_____

_____

_____

_____

TRUST: Everything you do and say must project your confidence in the vision, especially if you encounter a setback or temporary lack of progress.

- For example, "This is going to happen. It may not be easy. It may not happen as soon as we might hope. Nevertheless, it is going to happen."

- What are some things you can do or say to communicate your confidence and commitment that the vision is attainable?

_____

_____

_____

_____

PROGRESS: As you achieve milestones toward the vision, no matter how small, you need to share these achievements with others.

- For example, "Here is some evidence that we are making progress…"

- Regarding the vision you have established, what are certain indicators that will signal progress toward achieving the vision? How will you communicate these milestones?

_____

_____

_____

Actively Involved

> "Life is like riding a bicycle. To keep balance
> you must keep moving."
> — *Albert Einstein*

By definition, foundational networking is the process of developing solid relationships. You cannot do this by sitting back and letting the world operate around you. Foundational networking requires action.

You need to get out there and actively involve yourself. At work, if there are extracurricular projects to tackle or committees on which to serve, be at the forefront of getting involved. In your business, take the initiative of finding an industry association to join. In addition to your work or business, actively involve yourself with local school, civic and charitable organizations.

What is so special about you being actively involved? People want to associate with you when you are actively engaged in something beyond the daily minimum requirements. At these times, you transform yourself. When you become involved, you are no longer merely "someone" sitting on the fringe – actually or figuratively. You become a more central figure with very visible cares, concerns and goals.

When you set an example of action, you project yourself as a doer and a person of achievement potential. It is these prospects of success that attract others to you. From here, it is inevitable that your network will become more productive. This is because not only are you more accessible to others, but these others have a much greater interest in getting to know, like and trust you.

Understand, however, you cannot approach your involvement with the mindset of "just how much do I need to do" to project yourself as a person of action. If you do, you convey a "how little do I need to do to get by?" attitude. This serves to say, I am only interested in taking action to the extent that it is going to benefit me, a sort of quid pro quo.

Rather, your attitude needs to project a "what else can I do?" attitude. You need to look to take action. This casts you as an actively involved person, someone who sets an example for others.

There are no hard and fast rules as to what constitutes active involvement. There are certainly many levels of involvement in any setting, from the founder, initiator or visionary on down to the person who just works in the background to make it all happen. You should simply seek out a role that seems to suit you and pursue it.

Moreover, there is not a strict guideline that would dictate how actively involved you should be. Whatever the choice of involvement, the test of sufficiency is simple. You need to ask yourself this: Is my active involvement projecting me as someone giving more than the minimum required contribution?

If your answer is yes, your involvement is sufficient. If no, you simply need to become more involved and take more action. Setting an example of action requires that you go beyond the minimum.

More than 2,000 years ago, in the Roman Empire, a Roman officer under law could compel anyone to carry a load one mile. If the individual did not comply, the Empire could subject him to severe penalty.

Today, there are still certain requirements, such as compulsory school attendance until age 16. Although there are differences between the requirements of today and those of the Roman Empire, there is one thing they have in common: Each represents a bare minimum standard.

In reality, since the beginning of time, no one has amounted to much of anything by only doing the minimum. Behind any achievement and behind every success is someone who was willing to walk the second mile.

Consider the case of Francis Scott Key. He was not obligated to board a British warship during the War of 1812, the night he witnessed the Battle of Fort McHenry and was inspired to write the Star Spangled Banner. At the time, he was neither involved in the military nor a political figure. He did it because he chose to go the second mile and become actively involved in negotiating the release of an imprisoned civilian doctor.

If all we ever do is the minimum, then all we can ever expect is to obtain the minimum. You will not achieve success through foundational networking by expending the minimum effort. Setting an example of action, effort and achievement only becomes possible at the start of the second mile.

Foundational Networking Extra
An Example Of Action

After I left my consulting career in public accounting and started in private law practice, I joined the Ohio Business Brokers Association (OBBA). The OBBA is an association of business intermediaries, professionals that specialize in helping people buy and sell businesses, similar to a real estate agent who assists people in buying and selling houses.

Often these business intermediaries had clients who did not have attorneys. Thus for me – a young attorney with aspirations of growing a business law practice – this was a perfect networking opportunity.

Each month, I did the minimum. I attended the monthly luncheon. Beyond that, I did nothing with the OBBA or its membership.

Despite being the only attorney at these meetings, my membership and attendance yielded nothing. I gained no clients. I received no referrals. I came away each month with nothing. In fact, most of the business brokers did not even know my name – referring to me as "buddy," "big guy" or "counselor." This was, in and of itself, not a good sign.

After two years, I resolved to myself that this was not such a great networking opportunity. The timing could not have been better. My membership was up soon and I needed to re-submit my annual dues to continue it. I figured that I would not do this and simply let my membership expire.

However, before my membership was to expire, there was one more luncheon. As I had essentially paid for the meeting, I decided to attend, but I vowed it would be my last meeting.

This meeting proceeded like any other. However, at one point a member raised the issue of the organization's outdated charter and by-laws. Apparently, a select group of business brokers had started the OBBA six years earlier. At that time, these individuals simply threw together the organizing documents. Since then, the OBBA had grown. It was now at the point where it really needed to update these documents.

Shortly after someone raised this topic, every head in the room turned to me. While people may not have known, liked and trusted me as much as I would have hoped, at this moment in time I became the authority. As a result, the presiding President of the OBBA asked me to head up a committee to revamp the organization's governing documents. As I was too uncomfortable to say that I did not intend to continue my membership in the OBBA, I agreed.

I quickly renewed my membership for a reluctant one more year and got after the project of renewing the OBBA's by-laws. I organized a small group of experienced brokers to serve on the committee with me. Together we gathered up and reviewed the existing by-laws. We worked together to provide suggestions for changes and additions and presented these to the entire OBBA membership for their comment and review. With all this in hand, we drafted the finalized new by-laws.

Shortly after joining the By-Law Committee, things started to change for me in the OBBA. It started with my fellow committee members, but eventually infiltrated the entire organization. Almost immediately, in the eyes of the other members I went from being "big guy" to "Frank." They were getting to know me.

The business brokers started to realize that I was just like them: someone working hard to try to build a business and make an honest living. They could not help but start to like me.

Then, slowly but increasingly steadily, brokers started to rely on me for assistance. It may have started with small matters, but before long members were referring clients to me. I had established a growing trust.

Getting on the By-Law Committee was only the first of many activities I became involved with through the OBBA. For years, I was more than just a member of the organization. For years, I reaped the benefit of setting an example of action.

Eventually, as AmSpirit Business Connections grew, I stopped practicing law and I ceased being a member of the OBBA. Nevertheless, several years after I had ended my membership with the OBBA, I was still receiving referrals from business brokers I associated with through my involvement. In fact, even several years after I was no longer practicing law, a business broker called me to offer me a new client. Although I had to decline, this intended referral underscores the importance of being actively involved.

Situational Acceptance

> "A great attitude does much more than turn on the lights in our worlds; it seems to magically connect us to all sorts of serendipitous opportunities that were somehow absent before we changed."
> — *Earl Nightingale*

You should always be somewhat unsatisfied with what you have achieved or where you are in life. In so doing, you ensure that your greatest day is yet to come.

This attitude of high personal expectation is vital to your foundational networking efforts. With it, you project to the world that you want and are striving for more, which serves to endear you to others – they want to know, like and trust you.

Continually being unsatisfied is far different from being dissatisfied with your situation and circumstances. This mindset of dissatisfaction casts you as one who cannot help but blame your lack of achievement on your situation or circumstances. Expressing dissatisfaction is simply unattractive. Only others who are dissatisfied can identify with you and so few want to know, like or trust you.

You should always want more, but accept the circumstances and situations life has given you. In so doing, you need to understand two facts: Life is not fair and life is not perfect.

Life is not fair. You were not born on an even plane with the rest of the world, and even if you were, it does not stay that way for long. There are people who have more money and those who are better connected. There are people who happen to be in the right place at the right time. There are people who are not necessarily deserving of what they get.

In addition to not being fair, life is not perfect and it is not an endless succession of forward progress. Yes, there are times when everything is going well –

you are riding high and you feel virtually unstoppable. However, there are times when everything in your life seems to be off – the world seems to have conspired against you.

Yes, life is not fair and life is not perfect. So, you need to guard against allowing these troubling times to influence your attitude and outlook. More importantly, you need to ensure that these times do not alter how you interact with others.

In so doing, you need to bear in mind that as much as life is not fair, life is not unfair either. Generally, things are the way they are and that is just the way it is. There is no grand conspiracy against you.

Life is not unfair. You have had opportunities. They just may not have been the same opportunities as someone else. You simply need to go with what life has given you and strive for all you can with that.

Regarding the challenges you face in life, remember you are not alone. At one time or another, everyone experiences these. Furthermore, understand that your problems are no worse than 99 percent of the population – it just seems that way because you live with them.

Now, if you cannot keep these things in perspective, the next best advice is to keep your frustrations to yourself. You endear yourself to no one and do nothing to build the foundation of know, like and trust in your network by droning on like a four- or five-year-old with "it's not fair" or wallowing in self-pity.

In all honesty, no one wants to hear it. Although someone may listen to you, in reality, you garner no genuine sympathy. Eventually, these people will attempt to avoid you rather than be subject to your tedious monologues of perceived inequities and self-pity.

Everyone has perceived inequities in life and everyone has trials and tribulations. As a result, no one wants to listen to yours any more than necessary.

We all know someone who seems to be perpetually troubled with setbacks and perceived inequities. We ask them "How's it going?" and they treat the question as an invitation to vent incessantly about their personal and professional woes.

How do these individuals make you feel? They drain your enthusiasm. You seek to avoid them. If you cannot avoid them, you seek to minimize your encounters with them.

You refrain from introducing or referring them to others for fear that their disposition will be associated with you. If you cannot help but introduce or refer them to another, you find yourself later either making excuses for them or making comments in an attempt to distance yourself from them.

As you embark on foundational networking, you need to resolve not to be that person. Resolve not to be the person who is continually looking for someone with whom to share their issues and troubles. Do not be the person whom others seek to avoid or minimize contact with because you serve as a drain on positive energy. Ensure that you are not that person with whom others are embarrassed to associate.

Yes, life is not fair and it is not perfect. You must accept that and forge on despite it.

Foundational Networking Exercise

No one's situation is ideal and thus neither is yours. Nevertheless, what are the opportunities that the situation you have presents? Take an inventory of the great things about your situation.

_____

_____

_____

Foundational Networking Extra
The Crosses We Bear

Everyone has difficult stretches in their life. These are times when it feels as if the world has conspired against you and you cannot help but have feelings of self-pity.

While I cannot remember all the details, I do recall a period several years ago when I was in the midst of such a stretch – both personal and professional.

From a business perspective, nothing seemed to be going as planned. The only thing that I seemed to be able to count on was chaos and frustration (and from sources that I never would have expected).

At the same time, my kids were entering that age when they were becoming involved in various activities: Sunday school, soccer, Cub Scouts, Brownies, and a never-ending legion of birthday parties at bowling alleys and skating rinks. This was competing for what limited time I had.

On top of that, my wife and I decided that we would embroil ourselves in a tremendous kitchen-remodeling project. This was a further drain on my time and energy. Plus, it turned our entire culinary life on its ear – even toasting a bagel was an adventure.

On one particular Saturday, all of these elements were converging to put me in a foul mood. I was coming off a particularly stressful week and heading into one that was in all likelihood going to be no better. In between was a weekend when my wife and I were attempting to juggle kid activities with the next phase of our kitchen remodel. To add to the stress was the almost weekly realization that we were desperately low on certain staples, such as milk and cereal. This necessitated that we fit a trip to the store into our already chaotic weekend.

While I was not happy about it, I was off to the store with a shopping list in hand. The entire trip there I pondered to myself just how tough life had become. My mind vacillated. For a moment, I would be angry. Then I would allow my mind to consume itself with self-pity. "Is there anyone else on the face of the earth with the same troubled situation as me?"

As I arrived at the store, I could not help but notice a man preparing to leave his van and head toward the store. However, instead of moving toward the entrance as I was, he made his way to the back of his van and began unloading a specialized wheelchair using a winch and hoist system.

I slowed my pace and nonchalantly watched as the man maneuvered the wheelchair around the side of the van. He opened the front passenger-side door and carefully loaded his son into the wheelchair. From what I could tell, this man's son had a physical handicap and mental impairment.

As I followed them into the store, I figuratively walked in this man's shoes for a moment. Yes, my wife and I had to help our three kids get dressed each day, but we could look forward to the day when the kids could dress themselves (and then look forward to the day when all of their clothing choices would match). This man, however, was dressing his son each day with no hope of the situation ever changing. This was only the beginning of a litany of circumstances that I realized made his life more challenging than mine.

In fact, I could not help but conclude that my so-called problems were nothing but minor and temporary inconveniences. This was not a feeling of pity toward this man and his son. It was more a feeling of embarrassment toward my own thoughts and attitudes. I realized that my situation was not so bad at all. Overall, I have a good life.

Yes, I had challenges in business. None of them, however, were going to destroy what I had built.

Yes, the remodeling of our kitchen was throwing a kink into our daily lives. Eventually, however, we would have the project done. Plus, in the end we would end up with a more enjoyable home life (and besides, this was something we had brought upon ourselves).

Yes, we were chasing our kids around to lots of activities. However, our kids were healthy. That is a blessing in itself. Besides, kids are not kids forever. I realized that I should cherish these moments.

I was quietly, but sincerely, embarrassed. I was embarrassed for not only my thoughts and attitudes that particular day, but also for the other times I had similar thoughts and attitudes. I was embarrassed as to how these feelings of self-pity may have carried over to my interactions with others. I was embarrassed about the times when I commiserated with others about how tough my life was.

In short, that day I recognized that everyone has crosses to bear – problems and setbacks. While mine are generally no better or no worse than most anyone else's, they are not nearly as bad as some have it.

Courageous Determination

"The ultimate measure of a person is not where
he stands in moments of comfort, but where
he or she stands at times of challenge
and controversy."
— Martin Luther King, Jr.

You surely must know by now that there are certain realities upon which you can rely. One such reality is that life is not an endless succession of forward progress. While you may enjoy success, at some point or another you will encounter frustrating challenges and disappointing setbacks.

You may have experienced a missed promotion. On the other hand, you may have lost a key client. Additionally, you may have had a relationship that abruptly ended for no apparent reason. Whatever the situation, you have experienced frustrating challenges and disappointing setbacks.

It is during these moments of hardship that you have your greatest opportunity to engage in foundational networking. When you stare down these frustrating challenges and disappointing setbacks with an attitude of courageous determination you draw others toward you. These people cannot help but want to know, like and trust you more because of this mind-set.

When you meet with frustrating challenges and disappointing setbacks, life presents you with choices. You can completely withdraw and essentially quit, but would you want to associate with that type of person? The answer is probably no. You are no different from most people – they are not interested in associating with those who have given up or disengaged in some manner.

On the other hand, when you meet with frustrating challenges and disappointing setbacks, you can choose to become jaded and bitter. Again, do you want to associate with this type of person? The answer is probably a resounding "no." You have no interest in having the toxic attitude of someone else burden you, no matter how they came into it.

Finally, when you meet with frustrating challenges and disappointing setbacks, you can choose to resolve that you will find a way to overcome and then adopt the actions to make that happen. Do you want to associate with this type of person? Absolutely.

There is little question that people love an underdog. Further, they cannot help but rally around one who is battling to overcome some sort of setback or hardship. By demonstrating an attitude of courageous determination, you cast yourself in this light. Others want to draw from this strength and they hope to take inspiration from it. In any event, they cannot help but want to get to know you better and cannot help but want to get to like you more.

Foundational Networking Extra
Egg, Carrot Or Coffee

A young woman went to her mother and began telling her about her life. The young woman was in a time of great setback and challenge. She was tired of fighting and struggling. She wanted to give up.

Her mother took her to the kitchen. She filled three pots with water and placed each on a high fire. Soon the pots came to a boil. In the first, she placed carrots. In the second, she placed eggs. And in the last, she placed ground coffee beans. She let them sit and boil, without saying a word.

Twenty minutes later, she turned off the burners. She fished the carrots and eggs out and placed them in a bowl. Then she ladled the coffee out and placed it in a bowl. Turning to her daughter, she asked, "Tell me what you see."

"Carrots, eggs, and coffee," she replied. Her mother brought her closer and asked her to feel the carrots. She did and noted that they were soft.

The mother then asked the daughter to take an egg and break it. After pulling off the shell, she observed the hard-boiled egg.

Finally, the mother asked the daughter to sip the coffee. The daughter smiled as she tasted its rich aroma. The daughter then asked, "What does it mean, mother?"

Her mother explained that each of these objects had faced the same adversity: boiling water. Each reacted differently. The carrot went in strong, hard, and unrelenting. However, after it was in the boiling water, it softened and became weak.

The egg had been fragile. Its thin outer shell had protected its liquid interior, but after sitting through the boiling water, its inside became hardened.

The ground coffee beans were unique, however. The water did not harden the coffee and the water did not weaken the coffee. Rather, it was the coffee that changed the water – improving it … enhancing it … adding value to it.

"Which are you?" the mother asked her daughter. "When adversity knocks on your door, how do you respond? Are you a carrot, an egg or a coffee bean? Think of this: Which am I? Am I the carrot that seems strong, but with pain and adversity do I wilt and become soft and lose my strength?"

The mother continued. "Ask yourself, am I the egg that starts with a malleable heart, but changes with the heat? Did I have a fluid spirit, but after a death, a breakup, a financial hardship or some other trial, have I become hardened and stiff? Does my shell look the same, but on the inside am I bitter and tough with a stiff spirit and hardened heart?"

The mother paused and took a long, satisfying sip of coffee. Then, smiling, she proceeded. "Or are you like the coffee bean? The bean actually changes the hot water, the very circumstance that brings the pain. When the water gets hot, it releases the fragrance and flavor. If you are like the bean, when things are at their worst, you get better and change the situation around you. When the hour is the darkest and trials are their greatest, do you elevate yourself to another level? How do you handle adversity? Are you a carrot, an egg or a coffee bean?"

The point is that the happiest of people do not necessarily have the best of everything. The happiest, most accomplished people are that way because they just make the most of everything that comes their way.

Foundational Networking Extra
The Story Of Travis Roy

The sport of hockey is integral to Travis Roy's life. He first put on ice skates at just 20 months old and was deeply involved in the sport of hockey for as long as he could remember.

The summer before Travis entered the seventh grade, he went to hockey camp. At the camp, one of the counselors suggested that Travis make a list of hockey goals. That he did. He wrote down where he was and where he wanted to get in hockey.

Travis's list was an extensive one. Nevertheless, toward the end of the list, he wrote that he wanted to play for an NCAA Division I college, similar to his father who was a Hall of Fame player for the University of Vermont in the mid-'60s.

With the support of his parents, Travis sought the best competition to challenge his hockey skills and achieve his goals. As a result, his junior year he transferred to Tabor Academy in Marion, Massachusetts. While this change would require him to live away from home, the new school would provide him greater exposure to the recruiting efforts of NCAA Division I hockey programs.

The decision to attend Tabor Academy in the end was a wise one. Travis drew interest from several NCAA Division I hockey programs. Ultimately, he chose to attend Boston University, signing a letter of intent and accepting a scholarship to play hockey for the 1995 NCAA National Champion Terriers.

In the fall of 1995, Travis was set to achieve one of his final goals – play NCAA Division I hockey. At twenty years of age, on October 20, 1995, Travis entered into his first collegiate hockey game with less than two minutes having expired in the game.

Immediately after the face-off, Travis chased an opposing player into the corner after a loose puck, something he had done thousands of times before. This time, however, his feet became tangled up as he approached and he fell headlong forward. Within 11 seconds, Travis' life changed forever as he crashed into the boards and cracked his fourth and fifth cervical vertebra, paralyzing him from the neck down.

Travis Roy suffered a tragic setback, one that very few can begin to imagine. In the weeks and months following his injury, he certainly had difficult days, filled with anger, sorrow and frustration. Eventually, however, Travis adopted an attitude of courageous determination.

He engaged in an intense rehabilitation regime in both Boston and Atlanta, allowing him to regain some movement in his right arm. That year he returned to Boston University to become involved with his teammates' quest for another hockey national championship and then began attending class less than a year after his accident.

In 1997, Travis wrote *Eleven Seconds: A Story of Tragedy, Courage & Triumph*, which is now in its sixth printing. This book provides an account of how he realized his dream to play NCAA Division I hockey, how he managed through his paralysis and how he developed a determination to build himself for the future.

Travis graduated in four years from Boston University with a degree in public relations. In addition, Travis has become an articulate advocate for individuals living with spinal cord injuries. He is a frequent speaker on the need for increased medical funding in this area and the hope that continued spinal cord research carries. This includes testifying before a U.S. Senate Committee hearing for The National Institutes of Health in Washington, D.C. and the Massachusetts state legislature.

He founded and remains actively involved with the Travis Roy Foundation, a charitable organization that focuses on finding a cure for spinal cord injuries. This organization also provides grants to spinal cord injury survivors in financial need to help them purchase costly adaptive equipment necessary to live more active and independent lives.

Travis is also a popular motivational speaker. Speaking on topics such as "Conquering Life's Hurdles" and "A Change In Plans," Travis addresses corporate executives as well as school children from around the country on finding meaning and success in spite of the obstacles and setting goals and establishing values to make them come true.

More than 10 years after his accident, Travis continues to be an inspiration for others and a tremendous success. This all has occurred because in the wake of a terrible setback, he demonstrated an attitude of courageous determination. As a result, he draws to himself others who cannot help but want to associate with him.

Authentic Affection

"Let no one ever come to you
without leaving better and happier."
– Mother Teresa

An essential element of foundational networking is developing a habit of liking other people. After all, a part of the process of building know, like and trust in your network is having others like you. This will not happen if (even deep down inside) you do not have some small level of affection for them.

Remember, though, that everyone has something about him that can give you a reason to hold him in disdain. Conversely, everyone has something about him that can serve to endear him to you. It may be his work ethic. It may be a stance on a political issue. It may even be an allegiance to a particular sports team. In any respect, if you look hard enough, something is there for you to like or dislike.

Therefore, with whomever you encounter, you have a choice. Either you can find a reason to like them or you can find a reason not to. Given this choice, foundational networking requires you to adopt the attitude of wanting to like others and develop the habits to fulfill this.

Why is this important? Take a moment to picture someone you know – it can be anyone. Think about the qualities that can serve to endear them to you. In your mind, focus on these and put this person in the best possible light. How does this make you feel? It likely makes you feel good – a sort of warmth.

Now, imagining this same person, think about the qualities in them that you disdain. In your mind, focus on these and nothing else. How does this make you feel? You likely had a sense of contempt or anger welling up inside.

It should come as no surprise that whatever you feel tends to carry over into how you project yourself. After all, you cannot feel one emotion on the inside about someone and then effectively project something else on the outside.

If disdain is on your mind, this comes across (and others will have mutual feelings in return). If you feel a genuine fondness, then this is what you project (and others will return the feelings).

Given this choice, who do you want to be? You want to be that person with the attitudes and habits that consistently express fondness toward others – inwardly and outwardly.

To accomplish this, you first must adopt the attitude that you genuinely want to find a reason to like everyone. Then you should add to this attitude a genuine belief that each person has positive qualities that will cause you to like her.

With these attitudes, then you need to develop the habit of actively searching for those positive qualities that will serve to endear them to you. You need to endeavor to focus on these qualities, remembering them whenever you think about or encounter these people

In this process, you may happen to stumble across a trait or quality about these people that you do not find appealing. This is only natural. Remember, with everyone you can find a reason to like them or to not like them. When this occurs, however, remind yourself of their endearing qualities.

In any respect, this practice will give you the right mindset to develop a level of affection for everyone you encounter. Your affection then will carry over into how you project yourself. In short, people will perceive you as someone who expresses fondness toward others. In return, others will develop a fondness toward you, thus building know, like and trust.

Foundational Networking Exercise

List the names of a few people you do not particularly like. Beside each name, provide three or four likable qualities about them.

Person	Person	Person
_____	_____	_____
Likable Qualities	Likable Qualities	Likable Qualities
_____	_____	_____
_____	_____	_____
_____	_____	_____
_____	_____	_____

Foundational Networking Extra

Draw Your Own Conclusions

When I started in business, I found a small house to rent in the commercial district of old Gahanna, a suburb near Columbus, Ohio. Shortly after moving in, a friend paid me a visit. This particular person was a sales representative for a national provider of payroll services.

We met for a while, but as I walked him out to his car, he remarked, pointing to the office located in the house next to mine, "That accountant over there is a real jerk."

As I had just moved in, I had not met him and as I was still unpacking, it had not yet even occurred to me to go meet him. Therefore, the comment made by the payroll representative startled me a bit. Naturally, I assumed and hoped that I would be located amongst other friendly entrepreneur types. I almost reflectively asked, "Why do you say that?"

He was quick with an answer. "Whenever I talk to him, he is extremely short with me. During last winter when I stopped by to offer cookies to help him make it through the tax season, he threw me out."

I made a mental note. While I intended to be cordial, I needed to be somewhat cautious when it came to dealing with this particular neighbor. Short of me stopping over for a visit, though, it was not likely that he and I would meet any time soon. It was early February in Columbus, Ohio. The weather is gloomy and cold. Thus, there is very little reason to spend much time outside until mid to late April. Besides, he was an accountant and would be caught up until April 15th preparing tax returns.

Occasionally, when the timing was just right, we would see one another. As our offices were much too far apart to talk, we would simply offer one another a polite wave as strangers who are neighbors often do.

I kept in mind the comments made by the payroll representative – "That guy is a jerk … he threw me out of his office." I kept waiting to witness this behavior first hand. As I kept my distance, I did not expect that it would be unleashed upon me. However, I did expect to see him chasing people from his office or something similar. It never occurred.

When spring finally came, I arrived at the office one morning and the accountant was outside attempting to load a wooden canoe onto his minivan. I quickly gathered my things and moved from my car to my office door. As I was approaching the door, he noticed me and called out, "Hey, can you help me?"

I felt somewhat anxious as I walked over to where he was holding a canoe on its side. I attempted to play through my mind how I would react to all the possible things that might be said or occur.

However, the next thirty seconds were all business – that is the business of lifting a heavy canoe. Once we had positioned the canoe where it needed to be, we introduced ourselves and quickly got acquainted.

He was no longer the accountant next door, but Mike Hiland. Mike had been in Gahanna for 20-plus years. He not only worked in the house next to my office, but lived there as well. Over the years, he had built for himself a very nice accounting and tax practice and he seemed to know all the players in the established local business community. At the time, he was single and he had two kids who were grown and out of the house.

From that time, Mike and I seemed to see a lot more of one another. We seemed to be outside at the same times and we were no longer content giving one another neighborly waves across the lawn. We would meet halfway and talk or one or the other of us would stop by the other's office.

Whenever I encountered Mike, I could not help but reflect back to those comments made by the payroll representative – "That guy is a jerk … he threw me out of his office." I have to admit that I was leery of the situation for some time. I kept waiting for this side of Mike to show itself.

Mike had a friendly manner and his clients certainly seemed to like him. He never threw me out of his office, nor did I see him throw out anyone else. In fact, I cannot recall him ever raising his voice, other than to call me over to load the canoe on the minivan several times in the spring, summer and fall.

The truth of the matter, however, was that Mike was a wonderful ally. He referred me several clients and he introduced me to and networked me with many prominent people in the local business community. He also shared his business insights and flattered me on numerous occasions by asking for my opinion on matters pertinent to his business and personal life.

Unfortunately, one day Mike fainted. After a couple of tests, his doctor diagnosed him with cancer. Cancer specialists from around the country gave him only six to 12 months to live. Despite this, he endured a battery of experimental treatments in hopes of being a cancer survivor.

This was no doubt one of the most stressful times in Mike's life. His mind had to be swirling with a variety of thoughts and concerns … health insurance

... disability insurance ... business and client issues, which still had to be tended to ... issues related to family and friends ... trips to doctors and specialists ... stays in hospitals and clinics.

Mike remained Mike, however. I never saw anything that closely resembled the person my friend forewarned me about.

One day, I did share with Mike the initial impression that the payroll representative had given of him. In addition, I asked him if he had a problem with payroll services. He replied that he did not have a problem with payroll services and referred them whenever he could.

As for the payroll representative's comments, he made no denial. Rather, he offered a short, unapologetic explanation. "Those people ... show up unannounced at the busiest times and expect that you are going to drop whatever you are doing to meet with them."

Sadly, Mike did pass away after a courageous five-year battle with cancer. Although obviously not mentioned in his Last Will and Testament, Mike left me something when he passed. What he left me was a lesson.

With that in mind, just because someone has an unfriendly experience with another individual does not ensure that my experience will be the same or that the individual is unfriendly at all. Perhaps the perception of this individual was overcritical. Perhaps there were extenuating circumstances to the encounter, which would not affect my interaction with the individual.

Thus, when it comes to forming an opinion of others, I need to give them the benefit of the doubt. Moreover, despite what others might say, I need to draw my own conclusions when it comes to forming an opinion about people I meet.

Acknowledgement of Others

"If you wish your merit to be known,
acknowledge that of other people."
– Oriental Proverb

Imagine you walk into a business gathering filled with strangers. Who do you tend to gravitate toward, the person who treats you as a stranger by ignoring you or the person who takes the time to make eye contact and say hello?

Imagine you are in a meeting with individuals you have met before, but none of whom are extremely familiar with you. With whom do you feel most comfortable engaging in conversation, the person who addresses you by name or the person who obviously does not remember it?

Imagine you are at a social gathering involving your place of employment. Who do you feel the greatest affinity with, the person whose conversation with you is limited to business matters or the person who engages you in a conversation on matters of mutual personal interest?

You likely have an interest in getting to know, like and trust those who have an interest in you. Given that idea, you are extremely effective at foundational networking when you take an interest in others and work to acknowledge them in some way.

When you make an effort to acknowledge those around you, they want to get to know you that much more. When you make an effort to acknowledge others, they cannot help but like you as you make them feel important. When you make an effort to acknowledge others, they feel more comfortable about you and in the process are more trusting.

Therefore, you should make it a habit to greet everyone you encounter with eye contact and a friendly hello. This might make you feel a bit awkward at first. However, in time it will seem like second nature. Moreover, in time many people you have never met will perceive you as being an outgoing, friendly person.

You should also make it a habit to remember the names of those you meet. When you take the time to remember someone's name, you indicate to her that you value connecting with her. In addition, you subtly imply her importance to you. In short, these simple acts make the other person feel important, which serves to endear you to her. By just remembering a name, you serve to build the know, like and trust.

Beyond remembering names, endeavor to learn information about those in your network. You should learn about them personally, such as hometowns, marital status, children, pets, hobbies and affiliations. You should also learn about them professionally, such as educational background, work history and career specializations. The more you learn about them, the more the foundational networking occurs.

Foundational Networking Extra
Every Contact Has Opportunity

After I graduated law school and began working as a tax consultant, I had to drive each day into downtown Columbus, Ohio. While my car was nothing to brag about, it was my car. That was all the reason I needed to be somewhat particular as to where I parked it.

The owners of the parking garage I chose to park my car in, sought to maximize the number of cars in the garage each day. To do this, they instructed the parking lot attendants to have cars parked one behind another. This necessitated that those parking in the garage leave their keys with the parking garage attendant each day. This allowed the attendants to move cars as they needed.

At first, I was a little unsure about handing my keys to the parking lot attendant, someone who was a stranger. However, I quickly realized that I could park in this particular garage and not hand my keys over to a stranger. This was possible if I simply took the time to get to know the parking garage attendants.

This strategy did not require that I necessarily include these people in my circle of close friends or my holiday card list. Rather, all this strategy required was that I casually talk with them whenever I had the chance. From these conversations, I could learn their names, listen to what they had to say and learn something about them.

I interacted with most of the parking garage attendants. However, I spoke with one most every day. Her name was Twila. She spent most of her time near the board that held all the keys, so her location was a focal point of activity for everyone. For this reason, I generally talked to her in the morning when I dropped off my keys and then again when I picked them up at the end of the day. In addition, I might talk to her more than that if I had to leave the downtown area to go to meetings with clients.

To be honest, I cannot remember most of the trivial things we discussed in passing. However, I do recall that she had a daughter and a granddaughter and we talked about that. In addition, I remember that her daughter was involved in modeling with a local agency in Columbus and we talked about that as well.

One day, Twila told me that her daughter had heard that they were going to be shooting a movie 60 miles north of Columbus and that they needed attorney types to be extras. She went on to say that if I were interested she would get me more information. I thought to myself "why not." The experience might be fun. A couple days later, I got the necessary information from Twila.

The casting for extras was on the following Saturday, which gave me some time to plot and scheme. I got dressed up in a navy pinstriped suit on the morning of casting and had a friend take a picture of me in front of the wall of books at the law firm. Once finished at the one-hour photo mart, I was off to the casting at the old state prison in Mansfield, Ohio.

At that time, other than knowing that I was hoping to be an extra in a movie and that they were looking for attorney types, I knew very little. In conversations with others in line, I learned that the movie was based on a Stephen King short story titled *Rita Hayworth and The Shawshank Redemption*. I also learned that it would star Tim Robbins and Morgan Freeman.

I did not read much Stephen King, so I was clueless about the story line. What I know now is that the producers had taken a Stephen King short story and transformed it into a screenplay titled *The Shawshank Redemption*. In the story, Andy Dufresne (Tim Robbins) is a young and successful banker whose life changes drastically when the court convicts and sentences him to life imprisonment for the murder of his wife and her lover. Set in the 1940s, the film shows how Andy, with the help of his friend Red (Morgan Freeman), the prison entrepreneur, turns out to be a most unconventional prisoner.

While there was a courtroom scene in the movie, they did not have much need for attorney types. And so, those in charge of extra casting, in the irony of ironies, cast me as a prisoner. Thus, I took a day's vacation from my job as an attorney in downtown Columbus and spent it filming the scene in *The Shawshank Redemption* where Tim Robbin's character is first brought to prison.

The point is not to simply share my unique and wonderful experience – although it is somewhat humorous. The point is that every contact has opportunity. That is, we need to maintain the attitude that everyone we encounter has the potential to advance us, protect us or improve our lives somehow, some way.

This is not to say that every person we meet will be our next client. This is not to say that every person we meet will be our next employer. This is not to say that every person we meet has information that will save us thousands (or even hundreds) of dollars. This is not to say that every person we meet will lead us to a bit part in a major Hollywood movie. It does mean, though, that every person we meet potentially knows someone (who knows someone) who can.

Too often, we are prone to dismiss certain others as inconsequential to our lives. We quickly determine that they are unimportant to our well being or advancement. We have from time to time thought to ourselves, "He only answers the telephone and gets coffee." We may also quietly surmise, "She has no decision-making authority." In addition, we have possibly concluded, "She only is an attendant at a parking garage."

Twila was in no way directly connected to the production of the movie *The Shawshank Redemption*. However, through her daughter's connections, somehow she was. Of course, I did not know this when I met her. Nor did I expect anything from my casual daily connection to her other than a better than average care and concern for my car.

Every day, a couple hundred people came into the garage where I parked my car. Many of those people were attorney types just like me. Of all of them, I was the one person with whom Twila shared the information about the opportunity to be an extra in a movie. This was because I took the time whenever I could to acknowledge her and develop a relationship.

What the "every contact has opportunity" attitude advocates is that everyone we encounter – whether they are the person who takes our dry cleaning or the person who parks our car – deserves a certain degree of acknowledgement.

Sportsmanship

*"One man practicing sportsmanship
is better than a hundred teaching it."*
– Knute Rockne

There is no argument: Exhibiting sportsmanship is a good habit to have. The important point to make is that your ability to exhibit sportsmanship is not limited to games played on fields, courts and courses. After all, what is sport? It is simply athletic competition. Absent the athletics, it is merely competition.

As a human being, you compete every day, do you not? In your career, you compete to find a job, get a raise and obtain a promotion. In business, you compete to obtain an edge so that you can get (and then keep) customers or clients as well as have great employees. At home, you compete to have the nicer house or greener yard and to allow your kids to have the best possible opportunities. The entire human existence – like it or not – is about competing.

Any time there is competition (which is all the time), there are winners and losers … there is jubilation and frustration … there is achievement and disappointment. Given that, the habit of sportsmanship is vital to foundational networking.

Now, consider the time when you encountered someone who was not being a good sport, such as celebrating excessively when things were going well or behaving poorly in the midst of a setback. At that time, you had little interest in getting to know the person and you really did not like her (even if only temporarily). You likely did not get to the question of whether you trusted her. In short, there was no foundational networking.

However, when you exhibit good sportsmanship, you set a wonderful example that elevates your presence. Others are proud to know you. They cannot help but like you. Moreover, they want to believe that they can trust you.

Because of this, there are two general principles as to how sportsmanship must play into our foundational networking. One relates to when things are not going well (known as losing in the world of athletic competition). The other relates to the opposite end of the spectrum – when things are going well or when we are winning.

Principle No. 1:
Be Of The Same Character In Defeat As In Victory

Renowned author and speaker John C. Maxwell has remarked in several of his books that, "When we are winning nothing hurts; when we are losing everything hurts." This statement is so true.

Remember the last time that things were going well for you – you got a promotion or landed that prize client. You were almost giddy with excitement concerning your good fortune. In times like those, you tend to ignore all the little troubles that generally accompany life (minor financial or health concerns). This euphoria carries over in how you interact with the rest of the world.

The reality, however, is that life is not an endless progression of forward progress – accomplishment after accomplishment … achievement after achievement … victory after victory. Eventually you will endure a setback – whether as a participant, a fan or in the world of business or life.

How do you feel when things are not going so well? Your promotion went to someone else. You failed to land that prized client. Your star employee left for a competitor or client. Chances are in these moments your feelings are far from euphoric. In fact, whether or not you show it, you tend to take on a miserable disposition. In these times, your mind seems to magnify any little annoyance or trouble. Moreover, if you let it happen, you will thrust your dismal state onto those around you. You are stoic and less fun loving. You become distracted or preoccupied. You may even snap at someone for something that would not bother you at any other time.

"When we are winning nothing hurts; when we are losing everything hurts." Maxwell's statement is dead on. However, as accurate as Maxwell is, this does not mean that you need to accept it. It is only natural to experience a certain degree of disappointment and frustration with your setbacks and shortcomings. Nevertheless, there is nothing to say that you cannot fight to work through the effects of this discontentment and not allow it to affect those around you.

Here are four thoughts on doing just that:

- **Minimize The Effect**: Put the setback or disappointment in perspective. Just how vital is it compared to your entire life, business or career? The chances are that while it still marks a step backward from your goals, from an overall perspective the setback is likely relatively small.

- **Swallow Pride**: Remind yourself that the setback does not define you. It does not undo your prior accomplishments and achievements. In reality, all that has happened is that it has not allowed you to take a small step closer toward another goal. Therefore, you still have an entire body of work to be proud of.

- **Move Beyond It**: Remind yourself that your failure is not fatal. Everyone has failed. In fact, many of the people behind the greatest accomplishments throughout history suffered previous failures. As long as you are willing to pick yourself up and continue to pursue your goals, your greatest day is still yet to come.

- **Look For The Winning**: With every setback and disappointment, you gained something. It may be experience. It may be better relationships with those around you. It may be a better understanding of those who support you. You need to take an inventory of what you gained from your setback and truly appreciate it. This may be the best outcome to get you to your ultimate goals.

By working through each of these four thoughts, in the face of a setback or disappointment you will find that you hold yourself a little taller and prouder. As a result, others will notice this and they will be more impressed with you. They will be proud to know you. Their affection for you will grow. Moreover, they will believe that they can trust you.

Principle No. 2:
Remain As Humble In Victory As In Defeat

As I established in Principle No. 1, there is no great joy in losing. This is not a profound revelation. It is a humbling experience. Often the only way to describe the feelings of the disappointment is painful.

However, this pain fuels the euphoria of your achievements. The very real potential of feeling this pain makes you want to celebrate jubilantly when you achieve. You need to remember, however, that the world respects a modest winner as much as it does someone who loses with a demonstration of great sportsmanship.

This is not to say that you should not be happy and proud of your accomplishments. You should. Nevertheless, as with all things there are limits to the amount and manner you should celebrate. Remember, excessive celebrating and gloating does as much damage to how others perceive you as when you display a miserable disposition in the face of a setback.

Here are five thoughts to keep your celebration within respectable limits:

- **Have Perspective**: Put your achievement in perspective. While it serves to advance you, from an overall perspective it is likely small.

- **Appreciate The Past**: Each of your accomplishments is a culmination of lots of other accomplishments along the way. Without these lesser achievements, your current accomplishment would likely not exist. You need to take a moment to reflect and appreciate these.

- **Feel The Pain**: Whenever you have an achievement, there is likely someone else on the other end. Reflect on their feelings (and remember that there is no joy in losing). As everything in life is a competition, remember that the other person could have been you. Have some compassion for them.

- **Move Forward**: Remind yourself that just as your failure is not fatal, one achievement does not give you ultimate success. All that achievement generally gives you is the opportunity to work at a higher level. As such, quickly resolve that you need to continue the pursuit of your goals. Otherwise, you run the risk of failing at this higher level.

- **Look For The Lesson**: Every experience offers a lesson. With achievement, however, it is not so easy to find these lessons simply because you tend to wrap yourself up in the euphoria of the moment. Nevertheless, quietly consider what you learned from your accomplishment. This will help you temper your celebration and will allow you to earn more accomplishments in the future.

By working through each of these five thoughts as you accomplish and achieve, you will find that you will appropriately temper your euphoria. While you will impress others by your accomplishments, they will appreciate the humble nature with which you achieve them. Again, they will be proud to know you. Their affection for you will grow. Moreover, they will believe that they can trust you.

Authenticity

*"Be a first-rate version of yourself,
not a second-rate version of someone else."*
— ***Judy Garland***

To be successful with foundational networking you do need to focus on adopting the attitudes and developing the habits that project you as being genuinely happy, contagiously energetic, actively involved and all the other attributes covered in this section. Most importantly, however, you must be authentic.

When you are authentic, it means you are genuine and what you project on the outside is a true reflection of your thoughts and feelings on the inside.

This is important for two reasons. First, this is what people like about you. If you are an intense, take-charge person, you will attract certain people to you. You attract them because of who you are and they like you for that reason.

Certainly, you can endeavor to transform yourself — to be someone that you are not — in hopes of attracting a different cross section of people. This transformation, however, will likely alienate those who were once attracted to you. Be yourself.

No, you cannot always win — not everyone is going to like you. Even if some consider you to be the friendliest, most pleasant person out there, there are those who will detest you for it — perhaps considering you disingenuous. You can do nothing about this. Not everyone is going to like you.

Knowing that not everyone is going to like you leads into the second reason it is important to project on the outside what is on the inside: This is what you do best. If you are an intense, take-charge person on the inside, then you are best at portraying this. It is a perfectly natural role for you. When you exhibit something other than this, it will come across as fake or phony.

Be yourself. While you should hone the attitudes and habits that will make you more accomplished at foundational networking, do not feel that you need to take on the personality of someone else. In addition, do not morph yourself from one person to the next based on the setting and audience. It only tends to complicate matters as you will likely encounter the same people in different settings in different personas. Be yourself.

Foundational Networking Exercise

An important first step in being yourself is becoming aware of who you are on the inside. There are various proven and well-regarded personality assessment tools available on the market, such as DISC, Myers-Briggs, and LMI Profile Evaluation System. You should consider taking one of these. For now, however, examine the eight sets of characteristics below and determine for yourself where on the spectrum you are. This will be very insightful for you.

Impatient	1...2...3...4...5...6...7...8...9...10	Relaxed
Flexible	1...2...3...4...5...6...7...8...9...10	Rigid
Spontaneous	1...2...3...4...5...6...7...8...9...10	Planned
Introverted	1...2...3...4...5...6...7...8...9...10	Extroverted
Intolerant	1...2...3...4...5...6...7...8...9...10	Tolerant
Cooperative	1...2...3...4...5...6...7...8...9...10	Competitive
Sensitive	1...2...3...4...5...6...7...8...9...10	Tough-Minded
Trusting	1...2...3...4...5...6...7...8...9...10	Skeptical

Genuine Happiness

"You will find yourself refreshed by the presence of cheerful people. Why not make an earnest effort to confer that pleasure on others?"
– Lydia M. Child

You draw other people to you like no other time than when you are happy. This is because as humans we strive to be happy. As such, people want to know happy people, they cannot help but like happy people and they want to believe that they can trust happy people. Thus, a key aspect of foundational networking is to exhibit happiness.

Picture this situation. You walk into the room of a social setting and you are immediately engaged in a conversation with someone you know. That someone is carrying on in a jubilant manner. Almost immediately, you become more interested in him. You want to share in that joy, whatever it might be.

Then the mood changes, almost in an instant. He reveals to you that his apparent happiness is merely a temporary front for this event. He shares with you that his career is all but over and that his relationship with his spouse is in turmoil. At this moment, how do you feel?

Certainly, you do not abandon him. You are caring and compassionate. It is only natural that you want to be of some comfort. However, deep down inside you are no longer drawn to him. The mood has changed. You would like to remove yourself from the situation. This is only natural too.

Now imagine that you are the person with whom someone is coming to talk. You can draw the other person to you by being happy. You can repel him by being unhappy.

Exhibiting happiness or not is nothing more than an attitude. Moreover, it is up to you whether you choose to adopt a happy attitude. The most obvious means of demonstrating an attitude of happiness is to practice the habit of smiling.

As you interact with others, you need to do whatever you can to ensure that you have a cheerful disposition plastered across your face. If music puts you in the smiling mood, then you need to listen before you interact with others. If it is a good cup of coffee, sip away. If it is thoughts of happy times, you need to embark on daydreaming.

Of course, there are those times when you feel like nothing can make you smile. Not even the most uplifting song, not the freshest brew of java, not the happiest thought will give you the slightest grin. In those cases, the best advice is to smile anyway.

That is right. Even if on the inside you do not feel like it, you show it on the outside. Certainly, you need to be somewhat genuine about it. After all, after years of smiling, the muscles in your face will know what to do.

What is the benefit of this forced smile? Research shows that the mere action of smiling will change your disposition from gloomy to joyful.

In his book *Blink*, Malcolm Gladwell details the efforts of two scientists, Paul Ekman and Wallace Friesen, who created a catalog of facial expressions. They combed through medical books that outlined the facial muscles and made note of the distinct movements of each muscle. Then they began the process of understanding how people use these muscles in combination to create expressions. Ekman and Friesen ultimately – after seven years of work – assembled all these combinations into the Facial Action Coding System (FACS) and wrote them up in a 500-page document.

In the process of creating the FACS, Ekman and Friesen would sit across from one another for hours and attempt to recreate certain facial expressions, such as surprise, fear, happiness and disgust. At one point, they were working on anger and distress and had spent literally weeks attempting to mimic these expressions. In the process, they discovered that as they made certain expressions that their autonomic nervous system was causing them to feel that way.

As Gladwell describes what Ekman and Friesen claim, he states, "… the information on our face is not just a signal of what is going on inside our mind. In a certain sense, it is what is going on inside our mind." For example, if they forced an angry look on their face – even if they were in no way angry – they could actually detect feelings of anger and resentment welling up inside them.

This insight is not limited to negative expressions and emotions, however. It works on the positive ones as well. Thus, when you smile, you will begin to feel sensations of happiness. This is true whether you have an underlying reason to smile or not.

How does this all work? Who knows? Who cares? The important thing is that it does work. With this little tidbit of knowledge, think of the true potential or power of a smile. You walk into a room. Despite not having a particularly joyous day, you flash a smile. This smile is nothing extraordinary. It is one you would have, had you a genuine reason to smile.

Based on the findings of Ekman and Friesen, you almost instantly begin feeling like you should be smiling. Most importantly, everyone perceives you as being a happy person, which is a critical attitude in foundational networking.

So, smile and be happy.

Foundational Networking Extra
The House of 1000 Mirrors – A Japanese Folktale

Long ago in a small, far away village, there was a place known as the House of 1000 Mirrors. A small, happy little dog learned of this place and decided to visit. When he arrived, he bounced happily up the stairs to the doorway of the house. He looked through the doorway with his ears lifted high and his tail wagging as fast as it could.

To his great surprise, he found himself staring at 1000 other happy little dogs with their tails wagging just as fast as his. He smiled a great smile, and was answered with 1000 great smiles just as warm and friendly. As he left the house, he thought to himself, "This is a wonderful place. I will come back and visit it often."

In this same village, another little dog, who was not quite as happy as the first one, decided to visit the house. He slowly climbed the stairs and hung his head low as he looked into the door.

When he saw the 1000 unfriendly looking dogs staring back at him, he growled at them and was horrified to see 1000 little dogs growling back at him. As he left, he thought to himself, "That is a horrible place, and I will never go back there again."

All the faces in the world are mirrors. What kind of reflections do you see in the faces of the people you meet?

Unpretentious

"Be modest! It is the kind
of pride least likely to offend."
– *Jules Renard*

You are a great person. What you have to offer – your unique blend of
personality characteristics – is unmatched by anyone else. You need to
believe that and in so doing project an air of confidence, one that literally
attracts others to you. They want to know, like and trust you. However, the
moment that air of confidence crosses the line to an air of superiority, you
undermine whatever foundational networking you have done.

Take a moment and think about the last time that someone thought he was
better than you are, whether in his words or actions. It may have been
because of what he did. It may have been because of where he lived. It may
have been because of an affiliation he had.

Whatever the case, how did it make you feel? The perceived position of
superiority did not endear him to you.

The reality is that no one wants to associate with you when you carry on
as if you are operating on a superior plane. While you should have a sense
of pride about yourself (who you are, what you have accomplished and
with whom you affiliate), this does not make you better than anyone else.
Effective foundational networking requires that you adopt unpretentious
attitudes and down-to-earth habits.

Yes, forms of elitism abound everywhere. People in urban areas will remark
about the unsophisticated nature of "country folks." And perhaps, the
Harley-Davidson enthusiast will deem riders of any other motorcycle as
being a sissy. And, the fans of rival Michigan Wolverines and Ohio State
Buckeyes express a mutual disrespect for one another.

This elitist behavior, for the most part, is nothing more than good-natured
fun. It goes beyond this, however, if you truly believe that you are somehow

better than another based on your career, economic status or some affiliation, such as politics or religion.

You need to believe that you are great and that you have a unique offering to contribute to the world. Moreover, you need to feel a sense of pride toward your affiliations. At the same time, however, you need to possess and demonstrate the humility to recognize that everyone adds value to the world and everyone's affiliations are important.

It is true that market forces may assign a different value to the contribution of various occupations, professions and trades. Nevertheless, you need to adopt the mindset that everyone makes a valuable contribution to society. Moreover, it takes everyone's contribution to make everything work. The person who hauls the garbage is just as important as all the people who make those things that end up in the garbage.

Remember, biologically there is no difference between you and anyone else. We all have ten fingers and toes, 206 bones and the same basic DNA coursing through our veins. While you may want to argue that there are differences in levels of sophistication, this is superficial at best and probably completely irrelevant.

You should have a sort of personal swagger toward what you do – it is important and valuable to the fabric of society. As such, you should exude a sense of pride toward whatever you represent, whether it is a career, a religion or other affiliation. However, at the same time you must be deferential or courteous toward the affiliations of others and their pride in those associations.

Foundational Networking Extra
Just an Average Frank

One of the most successful people I know is Frank Carrino. He and I first met when we both arrived at the Columbus office of Coopers & Lybrand (now known as PriceWaterhouseCoopers) to begin employment as Associates in the tax department.

Within two years, the firm promoted Frank to Senior Associate and positioned him as a tax and financial consultant to the insurance and mutual fund industries. While he fulfilled his duties as a Senior Associate, he earned a Master in Laws in Taxation from Capital University. Eighteen months later, the firm promoted Frank to Tax Manager and started him working with other Coopers & Lybrand offices around the region servicing their financial services clients.

Within a year of becoming a Tax Manager, the rival firm of Ernst & Young attempted to recruit him away from Coopers & Lybrand. However, before Frank could make the transition, Coopers & Lybrand enticed him to stay. Within another year, though, Ernst & Young upped the ante and lured Frank to their firm.

Within two years, Ernst & Young promoted Frank to Senior Tax Manager and assigned him to consulting with Fortune 500 insurance companies and banks in Cleveland, Cincinnati and Columbus. But, before Ernst & Young could promote him to partner, one of Frank's clients recruited him – with a fantastic salary, stock options and a corner office – to work for them.

Frank Carrino is now the General Counsel and Corporate Secretary for the Westfield Companies, an insurance, banking and related financial services group of businesses headquartered about 40 minutes south of Cleveland. Frank is one of the top officers for one of the largest non-public companies in Ohio that provides commercial and personal insurance and surety services to customers in 28 states with $3.1 billion in consolidated assets. By any standard, Frank Carrino is a highly successful attorney, tax consultant and business executive.

What makes Frank Carrino such a success – the fact that he is a highly intelligent person? Certainly, this is an important factor. Frank is, without a doubt, incredibly intelligent. He could quickly make sense of passages in the Internal Revenue Code and has an encyclopedic knowledge of accounting standards and financial disclosure requirements.

However, this is true of most professionals who are hired into the large public accounting firms. These firms hire only the top students from the highest ranked accounting programs and law schools around the country.

Is Frank's success a product of his work ethic? Again, hard work is a vital element to success. At Coopers & Lybrand, I was a first-hand witness to the fact that Frank had an untiring work ethic. He arrived early, stayed late and frequently spent time during the weekend at the office.

Again, however, Frank was not alone. Public accounting firms are known for creating a culture of long hours and incredibly stressful work – especially during certain times of the year. No one lasts beyond a few months unless she is willing to adopt this work ethic.

Frank has an incredible work ethic and is highly intelligent. While these attributes have carried him far, they cannot account for the extraordinary success he has enjoyed. Then, what has?

The answer is that no matter what he owned or accomplished, Frank was (and by all accounts continues to be) unassuming. He was friendly and had a connection with almost everyone, from clients to vendors and from the firm's partners to those on the administrative staff.

The world of professional services (accounting, law, financial advising, etc.) is loaded with hard working, intelligent, successful people. Many devote a tremendous amount of energy to keeping up appearances ... projecting the appropriate image ... wearing the right clothes ... belonging to the right club ... driving the right car.

Then there was Frank Carrino. His suits were nothing special and he did not much care. He was not interested in golfing, let alone belonging to a country club. In addition, for years he drove an older model, two-toned beige and brown Mercury Zephyr – a box on wheels his friends called the "shoe mobile."

Beyond being unpretentious, Frank was supportive of some and empathetic with others. There were those he took under his wing. There were those he simply took the time to explain complicated issues or offer advice to. No one was beneath him.

Even with all the success he enjoyed, he continued to be approachable and down to earth. As a result, even though the firm billed hundreds of dollars per hour for his time, clients enjoyed the relationship. Moreover, to get the work done, he always had a loyal following of new associates who wanted to work with him and administrative staffers who were willing to go the extra mile for him. For these reasons, everyone wanted him on their team, which served to build his success.

Frank, intelligent and hardworking, enjoyed the rise to success almost immediately upon entering corporate America. None of this, however, made him better than anyone else. In his mind, he was just a person. He got dressed just like everyone else and drove on all the same roads. His abilities were superior in certain respects and inferior in others.

That persona, whether intended or not, served to make everyone around him always feel comfortable and never small or second-rate. Thus, the lesson from Frank Carrino is that a trip to the top requires that we consider ourselves to be nothing more than just an average Joe.

Personal Accountibility

"You can't talk your way out of problems
that you behave yourself into."
— *Anonymous*

Effective foundational networking requires that you adopt an attitude that is open to accepting personal accountability. This is not necessarily a natural thing, though. As part of the human race, you are hard-wired for self-preservation. Some people consider the practice of finding excuses, complaining and blaming others to be nothing more than a means of protection.

While it might be a defense mechanism held over from more primitive days, that does not make it acceptable behavior. In his book *QBQ: The Question Behind The Question – What To Really Ask Yourself To Eliminate Blame, Complaining and Procrastination,* John G. Miller addresses the notion of personal accountability. According to Miller, the Question Behind the Question is built on the observation that our first reactions are often negative.

For example, consider a situation when your son or daughter does not get the playing time you think he or she might deserve, your initial thinking might be "Why is the coach not playing my child?" Miller deems this an Incorrect Question, but it is only natural as it is not instinctive for you to blame yourself.

If in this moment you can instead discipline your thoughts to look beyond those initial questions and ask better ones – what Miller terms the Question Behind the Question (or QBQ's) – these subsequent questions themselves will lead you to better results. Returning to the example, rather than questioning why the coach is not playing your child, you would ask "What can I do to help my son do what is necessary to ensure he gets more playing time?"

Miller indicates that a wonderful habit you can develop that will ensure you improve your personal accountability is to simply replace incorrect questions (IQ) that begin with "why," "who" or "when" with ones that start with "how" or "what."

- **IQ**: *Why* do we have to go through all this change?
  QBQ: *How* can I adapt to this change?

- **IQ**: *Who* dropped the ball?
  QBQ: *How* can I contribute?

- **IQ**: *When* is someone going to train me?
  QBQ: *What* can I do to develop myself?

- **IQ**: *When* is someone going to give me the tools I need?
  QBQ: *How* can I be successful with the tools I have?

Yes, there are the days when your promotion does not come through or management gives it to someone else. The reaction should not be "Who will finally recognize me for my abilities?" Rather, the thinking ought to be "What can I do to leave no doubt in their minds that I am the best candidate for the next promotion?"

There are those times when you do not get the account you have been working to close. You should not commiserate with thoughts of "When am I going to get the sales support I need?" Instead, you should stare down defeat with a self-inquiry of "How do I ensure that I do close the next big opportunity that comes my way?"

By disciplining your thoughts to look beyond these initial questions and get at the QBQ's, these subsequent questions will lead you to better results. In addition to the benefit of better results, Miller's QBQ will also benefit you from a foundational networking perspective.

The person who laments her circumstances, makes excuses about failures or points the finger at others when things do not go as planned does not draw you to her. Rather, the person who has the courage to admit her failings and the willingness to venture forth and fix them intrigues you. Knowing this, you should adopt the attitudes and develop the habits that allow you to take command of your thoughts to ask yourself the "how's" and the "what's" as opposed to what Miller terms the incorrect questions.

Certainly, there are those who would argue that admissions of responsibility or accountability serve to repel others. These people conclude that others would naturally want to stay away from those who are prone to mistakes or faults.

However, the reality is that everyone makes mistakes. Therefore, if you admit yours, it does not serve to separate you from others. The mistakes are simply a validation that you are human and thus you draw yourself closer to others. They feel they know you better, like you more and trust you more completely.

Foundational Networking Exercise

Identify three situations in which you endured a personal or professional setback or failure. How would you best approach the situation from a perspective of personal accountability?

1. _____

2. _____

3. _____

Altruism

*"I expect to pass through this world but once.
Any good therefore that I can do, or any kindness that I can
show to any fellow creature, let me do it now. Let me not
defer or neglect it, for I shall not pass this way again."*
— William Penn

The second vital aspect of foundational networking, the developing of know, like and trust with those around us, works through adopting attitudes and developing habits of altruism.

What is altruism? In 1851, the philosopher Auguste Comte coined the French word altruisme with the meaning *"self-sacrifice for the benefit of others."* It entered the English language in 1853. More recently, however, evolutionary theorists, scientists exploring how unselfish behavior could have evolved, coined another meaning. Altruism is *"behavior that promotes the survival chances of others."*

In considering how this definition relates to your foundational networking, you need to reflect on the history of the human species. In the earliest years of human existence, people developed ways of interacting and ensuring one another's success. In short, they discovered they improved their chances of survival, as well as increased their level of prosperity, by simply sharing labor, tools and information.

Humans who hunted in an organized group were more successful than those hunting alone. Humans who shared labor produced more than those who did not. Humans who cared for and watched over one another tended to live much longer than those who operated independently.

However, chances of survival only increased if one was interacting with someone who was willing to contribute to the "greater good" of the community. If one were to contribute to someone who was never willing to reciprocate in some form or fashion, then his contribution would become a detriment.

Therefore, others would exclude from the social structure those who were not willing to contribute. Thus, those who were not willing to contribute became less likely to survive.

This could have occurred formally. In this sense, the individual may have been physically removed from the group or potentially worse. Alternatively, this excommunication may have occurred more informally. In this case, people became less willing to share with those non-contributors. Therefore, the non-contributor had no choice but to move on to another group, as survival ultimately depended on working with others.

While today it is not necessarily a matter of survival, but a matter of success and prosperity, the same basic principles still apply. Consider who you are interested in associating with more, the person whose attitudes and habits make him predisposed to contribute to the lives of others or an individual who cannot seem to part with anything?

The answer is obvious. You look to interact with and contribute to those who are willing to contribute to others. Success depends on this. If you contribute to another person who is never willing to reciprocate or contribute to society in general, you will find yourself in a worse position.

Thus, whether you realize it or not, you look for altruistic people. Everyone does. This is simply human nature. People want to know altruistic people. They cannot help but like them and it is much easier to trust those who have adopted attitudes and developed habits of giving to the world around them.

Once you understand and accept this idea, you need to endeavor to be that type of person. You need to become the person whose attitudes and habits focus on contributing to others. This is referred to as the Golden Rule of Networking and is quickly summarized as "give first; get second."

Donna Fisher, in her book *People Power*, refers to this as the "Boomerang Effect." According to Fisher, taking the initiative to give, participate and offer support to your network is similar to throwing a boomerang. Eventually what you inject into your network – opportunities, information, support, energy and additional contacts – comes back to you.

This is the essence of the altruism aspect of foundational networking. As you adopt the appropriate attitudes and habits and become more altruistic, you generate legions of people who want to know, like and trust you. While you do not expect it, these people will be eager to contribute to you as your altruistic attitude and habits will rub off on them.

This section will explore various aspects of altruism beyond how it is traditionally viewed – the transfer of wealth. In other words, what are the attitudes and habits that constitute altruistic behavior? Altruism is much more than just your action. Moreover, it is more than a simple mindset. It is a combination of both.

To gain a complete understanding of the various aspects of altruism, it is important to note that altruism is not an absolute concept. Rather, altruism is a matter of degree. Everyone has some modicum of altruism. Even the legendary Ebenezer Scrooge had altruistic tendencies, albeit few and far between. However, while everyone is altruistic, some are more so than others.

It is also important to note that not all altruism is created equal. Author Julie Salamon makes this point in her book *Rambam's Ladder*. In this book, she details the works of Rabbi Moses ben Maimon (known as Rambam), a 12th century physician, philosopher and scholar. As part of his teachings, Rambam identified eight distinct levels of generosity – the levels put together make up Rambam's Ladder.

Salamon acknowledges that every level of Rambam's Ladder constitutes generosity, but each rung up the Ladder constitutes a greater degree of altruism than the one before it.

A cursory understanding of Rambam's Ladder will be useful for you as you develop your own altruism to become more effective at foundational networking. More specifically, this understanding will allow you to gain a sense of which rung you stand upon (and it may be a different rung in different situations or at different times). This understanding will then allow you to advance your altruism to a greater degree.

Starting from the lowest rung and moving upward to heightened altruism, here is an overview of Rambam's Ladder:

1. **Reluctance**: In this situation, you give and are no doubt charitable, as you have parted with a portion of your wealth for the benefit of someone else. In your heart and mind, however, you are not happy about it. You give more so out of a reluctant obligation, a sort of "oh all right ... here."

2. **Proportion**: On this rung, you give and there is no reluctance in your gesture. However, the proportion of what you give relative to what you could have given is rather low.

3. **Solicitation**: This third rung of Rambam's Ladder is where most have their feet firmly planted. To garner your charity – even though you are willing to give in a reasonable proportion – someone has to ask you.

4. **Shame**: On this fourth rung, you actively are seeking to give without someone having to solicit your help. This, however, comes at a risk. That risk is that your unsolicited generosity serves to embarrass the person you seek to help. That is, the potential recipient either does not need the assistance or simply is too proud to graciously accept it.

5. **Boundaries**: In this situation, you contribute without being asked. The gift is likely significant, in light of your income or net worth. Moreover, there was little risk of you shaming the recipient as he is interested in the gift. You, however, want your name associated with the gift. For example, this might be a college scholarship or grant bearing your name.

6. **Corruption**: On the sixth rung, you seek to make an unsolicited contribution to someone you know. For whatever reason, however, you do not want your name associated with the gift.

7. **Anonymity**: On the seventh rung, you seek to make an unsolicited contribution on an unidentified basis. However, your contribution does not go to anyone in particular that you know.

8. **Responsibility**: This final rung is similar to the Chinese proverb "give a man a fish and he will eat for a day; teach a man to fish and he will eat for a lifetime." In this situation, you contribute to someone in a manner that empowers him so that he is in less need of future charity.

In summary, it is not a matter of whether or not you are altruistic. Everyone is altruistic. It is a matter of degree.

The other aspect to understand about altruism is that it is not limited to momentous acts. Certainly, large, meaningful acts qualify as altruism. These, however, are fewer and farther between than the minor, everyday actions you take.

Altruism is really an attitude that comes from the heart. Once you have the appropriate mindset, you will generally demonstrate your altruism in a series of smaller acts that consistently occur on a subconscious basis rather than through a few significant, well-planned actions.

A wonderful analogy or metaphor for this idea lies in the tale *The Story of Stone Soup*. This anecdote of a peddler's efforts to get a village to share its food is a metaphor for how simple acts of generosity can inspire altruism among a network of people.

Set somewhere in Eastern Europe, as the story unfolds a village is enduring a great famine causing the villagers to hoard whatever food they can find – hiding it from even their friends and neighbors. One day a peddler drives his wagon into the village. The villagers, not interested in feeding the stranger, encourage the peddler to move on, "We have nothing here for you – go to the next town."

The peddler, however, proclaims that he is not looking for anything from the villagers, but rather, he wants to share with everyone some stone soup. With a growing crowd of villagers watching, the peddler fills an iron cauldron with water and builds a fire under it. Then he ceremoniously draws an ordinary stone from a velvet bag and places it in the water.

As the stone broth simmers, the peddler moves the villagers to share their small, but hidden stockpiles of food. "Of course, stone soup with cabbage – that is hard to beat." Inspired to contribute, a villager retrieves a hidden head of cabbage and places it in the soup.

"Stone soup with a bit of salt beef, why that is fit for a king." Almost immediately, the village butcher eagerly produces some. And on it goes through potatoes, onions, carrots and so on, until everyone has shared. Before long, the stone soup is a delicious meal for all.

Like the peddler, who uses an innocuous stone to motivate others to give, your small daily acts of altruism serve as a catalyst for others. One small, well-intended act of altruism generally leads to another and then another. Soon, everyone is involved in a frenzy of generosity. Your simple acts of altruism – while inconsequential on their own – become contagious as you inspire others.

In this introduction, it is also important to discuss what altruism is not. Over the years, I have heard someone from just about every profession make a statement similar to, "I love what I do because I get to help people."

A great enthusiasm toward what one does is a powerful thing. It ensures that the business or profession serves its customers or clients at an exceptionally high level. However, when people look to serve those around them through the goods and services they sell – no matter how passionate they might be about the service – it is not altruistic. This is business passion.

In reality, this passionate servicing of clients is nothing more than sales or client service. No matter how much passion someone injects into the process of servicing customers and clients, this is simply providing someone pleasure or alleviating pain *through the goods or services she has to offer*.

True altruism in the foundational networking sense is not limited to what you have to sell and it is not contingent on a commercial transaction. It is doing something beneficial where you have absolutely no expectation of getting something in return, except for perhaps that warm and fuzzy feeling inside or the underlying belief that good will come to you in the long term. Thus, in contrast to sales and client service, in exercising your altruism you are providing someone pleasure or alleviating pain *through any means available to you*.

From a foundational networking perspective, when it comes to altruism it is not what you do that is important. What is important is rather how and why you do what you do.

Compassion

*"If you want others to be happy, practice compassion.
If you want to be happy, practice compassion."*
– The Dalai Lama

Although you may not have all that you want out of life, chances are you are better off than lots of people.

Take a moment and think about someone whom you have encountered recently. You need to pick just one person who was somehow disadvantaged or downtrodden compared to you. He may not have the connections that you have. Or, it might be that he may not have the same mental or physical ability as you. Or, it might be that he may not have had the same opportunities in life you have had. Whatever the case, in comparison to this person you feel fortunate somehow.

Now, take a moment and put yourself in this person's place. As you may have more connections, greater intelligence or better opportunities than this person, know that he has experienced suffering. Perhaps financially he is living on the edge of economic ruin. As such, he is distressed with the trauma of not being able to provide for his family, let alone get ahead professionally. And, perhaps this person's physical or mental disability prevents him from participating to the extent he would like.

Whatever the case, you should try to feel this person's pain. Attempt to identify with his challenges and stresses. Attempt to feel his insecurities. Attempt to understand his struggles, regrets and disappointments. Allow a genuine feeling of empathy to well up inside of you. This is compassion.

By allowing yourself to have these feelings, you will be able to develop a heightened sense of altruism. Whether you act upon this feeling is not necessarily important at this point. What is important is that you learn to develop the ability to look at almost any situation and feel compassion.

This is the key to infusing your life with compassionate altruism – developing the habit of looking around for those who have less or who are disadvantaged in some way. You need to have the mindset that no matter how dire your situation, there are others who have it worse. They are there. The chances are that you encounter individuals like this every day. You just need to look for them.

Once you have found them and you feel the compassion, you will more than likely find a means of – even if only temporarily – easing their heartache or bringing joy to them.

From a foundational networking perspective, you want to associate with the person who encounters someone who is less fortunate and allows compassion to take hold and somehow seeks to aid the situation, even if only in some small way.

Conversely, you do not want to associate with someone who altogether avoids the situation or, worse, takes advantage of the situation by attempting to profit from it.

You are drawn to the person who demonstrates compassion and so is most everyone else. Thus, you must endeavor to become that person.

Foundational Networking Extra
A Lesson from the Heartland

Have you ever heard of Brandon Teel? For many of us the answer likely is no. For some of us the answer may be yes. However, even if it is yes, we cannot exactly remember when or why we heard this name.

Brandon Teel received his 15 minutes of fame in December 2003. He did so not saving a family from a burning building. He did so not single-handedly raising a vast sum for charity. Actually, he gained fame by losing a junior varsity wrestling match.

Omaha, Nebraska sportswriter Craig Sesker wrote a story about Brandon Teel's loss, which appeared in the December 17, 2003 edition of the *Omaha World-Herald*. From there, ESPN picked up this story and reported it in its radio and television programming.

What was so special about this loss to motivate a sports reporter to write a story? What was so special about this loss to capture ESPN's attention? Omaha, Nebraska is certainly not New York, Chicago, Los Angeles or any other major metropolis, but then it is no small city either. The city and surrounding suburbs are comprised of close to three-quarters of a million people. There surely must be much more to report on than incidental losses in junior varsity wrestling matches.

Obviously, there was something special about this loss. And as Brandon Teel was the person on the losing end, he earned himself 15 minutes of fame.

In December 2003, Brandon was attending Kearney Senior High School and wrestling for the high school team, the No. 2-ranked team in the state. As a senior for the Bearcats, he was a backup in the 189-pound weight class.

One day, the Bearcat wrestling coaches approached Brandon with an unusual request. It all started when the head wrestling coach for the Lincoln East Spartans, a nearby rival high school and No. 1-ranked team in the state, e-mailed Brandon's coach with a request. The Lincoln East coach asked his counterparts at Kearney if one of their wrestlers would compete in a junior varsity match against one of the Spartan wrestlers.

The request was unusual because the Spartan wrestler was a freshman named Trevor Howe. This Lincoln East freshman has Down syndrome, a chromosomal disorder resulting in mental retardation and an inability to fully develop motor skills. Thus, for Trevor wrestling was a struggle.

The Kearney coaches agreed to find someone to wrestle the East Lincoln High freshman. They knew that it was going to take a special kid for this situation, so they quickly decided to ask Brandon Teel to take on this challenge.

However, the challenge was not in winning the match. Under normal circumstances, an experienced senior would be too much for a freshman. And under these special circumstances, Trevor did not stand a chance against Brandon.

The challenge was in the stipulations placed on the match. The coaches asked Brandon not to pin Trevor for two periods as well as not hurt him. The Lincoln East coaches just wanted Brandon to let Trevor experience wrestling in a competitive match.

Brandon accepted his role. Additionally, Brandon further agreed that he would not pin Trevor at any point during the match. Rather, Brandon would allow the match to proceed for a full six minutes and he would beat Trevor on points.

For a young competitive athlete at a wrestling powerhouse like Kearney Senior High School, Brandon's agreement to allow Trevor to remain competitive was noble in and of itself. If the story were to stop here it still might even be worthy of an article in the *Omaha World-Herald* and a mention on ESPN. However, it did not end there.

Once the wrestling match began, something happened to the Kearney Bearcat senior. Brandon Teel was overcome with what can be described as a tremendous wave of class, generosity and compassion. Picking the appropriate time, Brandon allowed himself to be pinned, giving the victory to the freshman.

"He was really working – he was trying so hard," Brandon told the *World-Herald* reporter. "I was supposed to win on points in the third period, but I didn't think it would be right for me to beat him. It ended up being better this way anyway."

When the referee declared victory for Trevor, the entire gymnasium erupted. Trevor jumped up and down. He hugged his coach. He hugged his dad. Both wrestlers received a standing ovation. Brandon received accolades for his sportsmanship.

On Saturday, December 13, 2003, 17-year-old Brandon Teel gave Trevor Howe something he might not otherwise have had – the thrill of a lifetime to step onto a wrestling mat and earn a victory. He gave Trevor's parents something that they might never have expected. He gave all those in attendance a wonderful experience – the sheer joy of one person's unlikely triumph. And Brandon Teel gave us all a lesson.

The lesson is that moments of great compassion do not find us. Rather, we find them. Brandon did not have to lose. He did not have to allow himself to be pinned. He could have done exactly what the coaches had agreed – give Trevor a hard fought experience, not hurt him and take the victory in the third period – and no one would have thought less of him. Rather, Brandon chose a nobler course. He saw an opportunity to exercise great compassion and he took it.

More importantly, consider this: Brandon Teel was just a 17-year-old kid competing in an obscure junior varsity wrestling match somewhere in small town Nebraska. If he could find an opportunity to exercise great compassion, it should not be that difficult for us to do the same, considering we are mature adults, dealing with real world matters with metropolitan connections.

Encouragement

"We rise by lifting others."
– *Robert Green Ingersoll*

When people think of altruism, they generally think of one idea – the act of giving tangible objects, such as money or property. Far too often people have this limited mindset of altruism.

One aspect of altruism that seldom gets much consideration is the notion of providing someone else with moral support. There is tremendous value in pouring ourselves into picking others up when they are down.

The road to a happy and successful life – whether personal or professional – is not an endless progression of forward progress for anyone. Even the most successful people have endured setbacks and failures at one point or another, and they will happily share their stories of overcoming hardship. And, in sharing these stories, each of these people will cite someone as being their moral support during challenging times. It may have been a parent, a teacher, a coach or a friend. Whoever this person is is not important. Of importance is that the person comes along and provides the needed encouragement or uplifting spirit.

Everyone around you will eventually endure some degree of adversity and face a certain amount of setbacks. Those around you will fail to convert prospects to a client. Some will fail to make a personal relationship work out. And they will fail in countless other ways as well.

While you too are prone to failures, you can use the failures of others to become altruistic and thus aid in your foundational networking. You do this by resolving to help others stare down failures as well as learn from their mistakes and move forward with perseverance.

In so resolving, you need to develop an arsenal of techniques and approaches to help others rekindle their will after a setback. Here are some techniques and approaches to include in your arsenal:

- **Provide Reassurance**: You can remind others that the failure is not a reflection on them (they are not failures), but merely an indication of something that they attempted to do (what they attempted to do failed). For example, say something like this:

"So you did not get the engagement. You are great at preparing and presenting proposals. That is a fact. This particular opportunity simply did not work out for you. You can still build on and learn from this experience."

As John C. Maxwell indicates in his book *The Success Journey*, "as time has gone by, I've learned to accept my limitations as well as my strengths, understanding that everything I do isn't going to be successful and tell myself, 'I sure messed that up. I'll do better next time.'"

- **Reflect on Success**: You can remind others that while the failure did occur, they need not take it personally and they should reflect on all the positive things they should be proud of and take credit for. For example, say something like this:

"No, you were not successful in closing the deal. That is all right. Up until now, you have had a good track record closing and the ones you have closed are extremely profitable. One sale will not make us; one sale will not break us."

- **Share Stories Of Other Failures**: You need to remind others that everyone experiences failure from time to time, even you. You can do this best by sharing stories of your own setbacks or the failures that others have experienced. In so doing, you can illustrate how you or others worked through and eventually benefited from these disappointments. For example, say something like this:

"Do not be discouraged. When I was just getting started, I had a similar setback. It was discouraging, to say the least. But I kept after it. Now look at me."

In his book, *Bringing Out The Best In People*, Alan Loy McGinnis indicates that "we must dispel from our minds the idea that successful people never fail. Successful people make as many and as ghastly mistakes as everyone else. The difference is that successful people admit them, laugh at them and learn from them. That is, in part, how they got to be successful."

- **The Glass Is Half Full**: You need to challenge others to view the failure in its most positive light. For example, say something like this:

"Yes, you wanted to get that promotion. While you may have fallen short of that goal, the effort you put forth in the process has made a lot of people in this company stand up and notice you. I would not be surprised if other opportunities – even better opportunities – come your way."

- **Focus On the Future**: Generally speaking, the failures of others "are water over the dam." That is, any potential damage, whether large or small, has been done. Dwelling on the failure and the impact that it may or may not have is generally pointless or only serves to exacerbate the problem. You can move others forward best by focusing them on their next move.

In her book *Ten Things I Learned From Bill Porter*, Shelly Brady indicates that the attitude of Bill Porter is that it doesn't matter how we get to our place in life, but only where we are headed. Born with cerebral palsy, Porter overcame this obstacle to become the renowned, all-time champion door-to-door sales representative for Watkins Products. For him, the past is the past and it cannot be changed. Rather than dwell on what might have been, energies are best focused on moving forward.

Certainly lifting someone up when he is down is not the act of giving tangible objects. It provides no direct or indirect immediate enrichment. Nevertheless, there is tremendous value in providing someone else with this moral support, value you should consider altruistic.

Failures, setbacks and disappointments are inevitable. So the question is not whether or not those around you will experience them. The question is whether and to what extent, you will use these failures as an opportunity to undertake some foundational networking.

Foundational Networking Extra

The Arsenal

Over the past several years, my kids have been involved in travel soccer. These are teams that are comprised of kids with an interest in playing soccer on a serious level and acumen for doing so. The team my kids play for is known as the Arsenal of the Gahanna Futbol Club. The various teams of the Arsenal travel around the central Ohio area playing select teams in their appropriate age group from other local communities.

The first year my oldest son, Lucas, was involved with the Arsenal, he decided that he wanted to share the duties of playing goalie with another boy on the team. Although they each had the opportunity to play other positions during the game, for one half of the game my son would play goalie and the other half the other boy would take on these responsibilities.

Like any young boy or girl participating in youth sports, Lucas has had good days and he has had bad ones. However, there was one particular match in the year-end tournament during his first season of soccer where things became simply terrible.

The team the Arsenal was playing this particular match was simply a better team. Their kids were bigger and faster, more physical and more skilled than our kids. Although the Arsenal did all it could to keep pace with this other team, it was only a matter of time before the kids would wear down. While the second half started with the Arsenal only down 2-1, midway through the half the Arsenal yielded to superior size and skill.

As the situation turned out, Lucas was slotted to play goalie during the second half of the match. This was not a particularly good time to be in goal as Lucas was peppered with shots and forced to defend a string of breakaways. Although he, like the rest of the team, made a valiant effort, in the end he gave up five goals. After the first two goals, my then eight-year-old son was dejected. Goal three, four and five sunk him toward being devastated.

After teams shook hands, I met up with Lucas on the field. He stopped and looked at me with his little long face. I got down on a knee to hug him and as I did, he started to cry. We just stayed there for what seemed like a couple minutes. Although different in some respects, it was a moment that all parents endure with their kids at some point or another. You want to take the pain away, but you just do not know how.

Then out of nowhere, Lucas' coach, John Grimme, came over and knelt down beside us. He patted my son on the back and reassured him that he had played a good game. He went on to share with Lucas that three or four of the goals were not his fault. He explained that long before the other team got their shots, his teammates had a half dozen other breakdowns along the way. He shared with Lucas how his older son, who was also a goalie, had been put in the same predicament just a few days before.

As for the shot or two that Lucas should have stopped, Coach Grimme gave him some quick advice as to what Lucas should do next time. Mostly he simply reminded Lucas to use those goals as a learning experience.

At that point, Lucas did not stand up and walk away dry-eyed and smiling. However, the reassurance and encouragement provided by his coach helped him stare down a setback. That afternoon, in the very next game, Lucas was back in goal with a confident swagger as if the morning debacle never occurred.

Smiles

> "Today, give a stranger one of your smiles.
> It might be the only sunshine he sees all day."
> Quoted in P.S. I Love You, compiled by
> *– H. Jackson Browne, Jr.*

What is the one thing you can give that makes you happy and makes others happy and yet it costs you neither money nor time? The answer is a smile.

What is so special about giving smiles? When you smile, people tend to smile with you. According to an article published in the *Journal of Psychophysiology* ("Facial Expressions Are Contagious", 1995, L. Lundquist and U. Dimberg), researchers found a tendency for subjects to mimic the expressions of those around them.

Thus, if you encounter someone and you start laughing, she will likely join you – even though she has no idea what the source of the humor was. If you have a serious look on your face, she becomes stoic. If you encounter someone and you are smiling, she will certainly begin beaming from ear to ear.

I see an example of this in my own neighborhood. There is a little boy who reminds me of those smiley face buttons and T-shirts that were part of the popular culture of the 1970s. He seems to have a permanent smile on his face. Whenever I see him, he is genuinely smiling from ear to ear. Riding his bike on the street, he is smiling. Playing ball, he is smiling. When his mother hustles him off for dinner, he is smiling. I am sure he has his moments – just ask his parents. Nevertheless, whenever I see him he is smiling.

Beyond the fact that he is always smiling, what I have noticed is that whenever I see his smile, I cannot help but smile. No matter how bad my day may have shaped up, he can change my entire mood by smiling, usually as he comes running up asking, "Hey Frank, can your kids come out and play?"

Mimicking the expressions of others – particularly smiles – is a normal human reaction. When we give someone a smile, we cause him or her to smile.

Again, however, what is so special about giving smiles? As you learned in the chapter titled "Genuine Happiness" in the Presence section, research has shown that when people smile – whether real or forced – a physiological reaction in their brains causes them to be happy.

Thus, when you give a smile, people smile back and this makes them feel good. From there the lesson is simple. People want to associate with those who make them feel good.

Foundational Networking Exercise

Develop a list of five things (items, songs, or thoughts) that are sure to bring a smile to your face. Keep a copy of this list handy (at your office, in your car, or with you somehow).

1. _____

2. _____

3. _____

4. _____

5. _____

Volunteerism

"Volunteers are not paid not because they are worthless, but because they are priceless."
– Unknown

Altruism is much broader than transferring wealth. In addition to compassion, encouragement and smiles, you can also give others your time.

Consider any local community program, non-profit organization or grade school. Each and every one is stretched beyond its resources on every front. While financial contributions are always welcome, what they desire most is your time, talents and experiences. They want you to volunteer.

Your natural response to this might be, "Volunteer!? That provides nothing other than a distraction or drain on my limited time."

While this is an understandable response, it is not an accurate depiction of what volunteerism has to offer you. Primarily, volunteering is an opportunity to exhibit your altruism and further your foundational networking. Thus, your time spent volunteering serves to make others want to know you, like you and trust you.

In addition, another reason that volunteering is neither a distraction nor an unproductive consumption of your personal and professional time is that it offers as much as you give it and, even better, you get the benefits now.

Consider this, as an ambitious person, you continually strive to enjoy more success – make more money or advance yourself. To achieve this success, you want two things. Whether you are a self-employed entrepreneur, high-level executive or rank-and-file peon, you simply want an opportunity and an advantage.

With an opportunity, you could prove yourself. You could prove that you are able to manage, motivate and lead others. You could prove that you have strong organizational skills. You could prove that you can effectively communicate. You could do all this, if only somehow you could get an opportunity.

With an advantage, you could separate yourself from the competition. You could have a "leg-up" when it comes time to make promotions. You could be positioned to close that key account. You could garner those accolades you have dreamt of. You could do all this, if only somehow you could get an advantage.

Opportunity. Advantage. If you had either or, better yet, both, you could not only realize greater success, but the income that comes along with it. But neither opportunities nor advantages are easy to get hold of.

Opportunities only seem to be given to those who have proven themselves. In short, you miss so much because there is so much you have not done. Which begs the question, without the opportunities how do you initially prove yourself?

Gaining an advantage is something you dream about, hope for and work into your strategic plan. Then reality sets in. In the heat of the daily battle, it is difficult to focus on achieving an advantage when you are continually consumed with simply holding the ground you have.

Perhaps this is what makes success so special – because the two vital components of success are so hard to obtain. Or are they? While there may be a dearth of these ingredients in your business or on the job, they are all around you. Where? Simple. A plethora of opportunity and advantage exists day in and day out by simply volunteering.

Want an opportunity to manage others, but there is no occasion to do so with what you are doing now? Looking for an opportunity to hone your communication skills, but there is little chance of doing so in your current situation? What about opportunities in strategic planning, financial management, team building or event planning? No problem. While each volunteer position does not provide every potential opportunity, pretty much any opportunity you desire can be found somewhere in volunteering.

How would these opportunities translate to your job or your business? Perfectly. Skills are skills and experiences are experiences. It matters little where you obtain them.

Certainly, with these opportunities come new experiences. And with these new experiences you instantly create an advantage over the next person. But the advantage of your little acts of altruism goes further than the know- how you gain.

When you volunteer, you are not doing so all alone. When you volunteer, you pull yourself out of your own little world to work with others who are doing the same. These are people you otherwise would not have known but for your mutual willingness to give your time and talents.

These new contacts fortify and diversify your network. Instantly your professional value increases, as these people will connect you to potential clients, business partners and employers. Additionally, these new contacts will provide you new ideas and information. Finally, your interaction with them stimulates ambition as you benchmark yourself against new and interesting people. All of these experiences distinguish you from your contemporaries. That, in and of itself, creates an advantage for you.

The benefits of volunteering, however, go beyond enhancing your skills and fortifying your network. Study after study shows that by volunteering you become happier and healthier than those who do not.

For example, researchers at Cornell University determined that volunteering boosts self-esteem and energy. In the process, it offers you a sense of mastery over your life and gives you a sense of yourself as engaged in meaningful, productive activities that help change the world, which benefits your psychological well-being. Additionally, a study at the University of Michigan demonstrated that people who volunteer are more likely to live longer.

Volunteering: It is an essential ingredient of foundational networking. It offers you an opportunity to build your experience and give you an advantage by introducing you to new and interesting people. In addition, it will give you a longer, healthier life. These benefits certainly serve to have a positive impact on your personal and professional success.

Foundational Networking Exercise

What are three organizations that you are or would like to become involved with?

1. _____

2. _____

3. _____

Compliments

"I can live for two months on
a good compliment."
– *Mark Twain*

Everyone has drive. Whether you are self-employed or gainfully employed, you are driven to have more than you did and to be more than you are.

Generally, your compensation for this drive comes in the form of the rewards associated with advancing yourself. You make more money. You gain greater control of your situation. You have more security. You have more leisure time. You simply feel better about yourself.

These are the intrinsic benefits. Beyond these built-in benefits, however, you also take great satisfaction in having others recognize you for the fruits of your drive. In short, you receive a certain amount of enjoyment out of having someone say to you:

• You did a great job managing your team this year.

• You have an impressive service.

• You look the same as you did in high school – Great.

These are compliments or words of congratulations. Items like a promotion, a raise or better clients are important to sustaining you. These personal accolades, however, serve to build your spirit. Therefore, it is easy to conclude that giving compliments is an act of altruism.

When you tell someone, "WOW, you have lost weight and look great," you immediately spur them on to continue with whatever diet and exercise program they are on in pursuit of shedding the next 5 or 10 pounds.

Compliments require no great skill and you did not need any money or much time with which to give them. Therefore, you should never be at a loss for ways to be altruistic as these positive acknowledgments certainly serve the purpose.

As Susan Jeffers states in her book *Dare To Connect*, "the purpose of the compliment is not to make [others] like you, but rather to enrich their lives in some way." In short, complimenting is altruistic. This is simply a matter of focus and habit. In other words, if you put forth a sufficient, sustained focus on giving compliments, eventually it becomes a habit.

You need to remember that there is no rule that says compliments must flow from the top down. Compliments can and should run in any direction. Therefore, you can give your bosses, clients and parents the accolades they deserve. You can simply make comments like … "You are a great client to work with." … "I appreciate the opportunities you have given me." … "Mom and Dad, I hope to give my kids the support and encouragement you provided me."

Therefore, whether you are most comfortable sending compliments flowing top-down, bottom-up or side-to-side, it is likely that the accolades you provide will come back to you. Nevertheless, in no time, no matter what comes back to you, you will have developed a new altruistic habit.

Foundational Networking Exercise

If you are looking to get into the habit of giving more compliments, follow the advice of Andrea Nierenberg. In her book *Nonstop Networking*, Nierenberg recommends that until you get in the habit of giving daily compliments you start each day with five pennies in your right pocket.

Each time you give a compliment or offer up some genuine praise, you simply shift one penny from your right pocket to your left. Obviously, the objective is to end the day with all five pennies in your left pocket. In time, giving compliments will be a wonderful altruistic habit that will serve to advance your foundational networking.

Foundational Networking Extra
The Elevator Principal

In his book *Winning With People*, John C. Maxwell refers to compliments, accolades and the notion of adding positive energy into the lives of others as "The Elevator Principle." In starting out this section, Maxwell shares the story of George W. Crane, a physician, consultant and psychologist.

In the 1920s, Crane taught social psychology at Northwestern University in Chicago. One particular class was comprised of individuals who were older than the average college student. These men and women went to class at night and by day worked in department stores, offices and factories in the Chicago area.

Crane came up with what he called the Compliment Club as the class' first assignment. Every day, for thirty days, according to Crane each student was to "pay an honest compliment to each of three different people … then, at the end of the thirty-day experiment, I want you to write a theme or paper on your experiences." He wanted them to include in their papers changes they noted in the people around them as well as their own altered outlook on life.

He lectured them that there was opportunity for praise and compliments all around them, stating, "You will find that nobody is entirely devoid of merit or virtue." In other words, no matter whom we are dealing with – whether a close friend or a sworn business combatant – we can find something to praise them for in a sincere manner.

According to Crane, his students discovered that their sincere compliments had a positive impact on the people around them. This is not completely surprising – praise, accolades and congratulations contribute to the lives of others.

According to Maxwell, the "Elevator Principle" states that "we can lift people up or take people down in our relationships." Crane's Compliment Club was simply giving his students a proactive approach to this principle. There should never be a dearth of compliments, especially knowing the benefits to others and the relative ease of giving them.

Appreciation

"Appreciation can make a day, even change a life. Your willingness to put it into words is all that is necessary."
— Margaret Cousins

An expression of appreciation has likely been part of your entire speaking life. Almost universally, the first words your parents endeavored to teach you to say were "mama" or "dada." Shortly thereafter, your parents attempted to grow your young and impressionable vocabulary, while making you a polite human being, by teaching you to say "thank you" or some other words of appreciation.

Although your first "thank you" was likely for something given to you, you now realize that there are many reasons to show your appreciation. If someone gives you a compliment, you thank her. If someone buys you lunch, you thank him. If someone gives you a referral, you thank her. In short, it is hard to identify a situation in which you do not have an opportunity to express your genuine and sincere appreciation.

- You can express gratitude for encouragement. "I truly appreciate your support. It has meant a lot over the last few days."

- You can express appreciation for someone's friendship: "It is really nice to have a friend like you. Thanks."

- You can even thank someone for thanking you: "I appreciate you taking the time to express thanks to me. That makes me feel good."

Although you probably spoke your first "thank you," you now also know that there are as many ways to express appreciation as there are things to be thankful for. Clearly, you can continue to verbally say thank you – whether in person or over the telephone. You can say thank you in a note – whether handwritten or typed. You can say thank you by returning a favor – whether a similar favor or something entirely unrelated. You can say thanks by sending a gift of appreciation – whether something meaningful or a small token.

The "when's" and the "how's" of saying thanks are reasonably clear. Your parents taught you to say it with the intent of setting you on the path to being a courteous, well-mannered human being. In short, you say thank you simply because it is the right thing to do. Despite these intentions, by laboring to teach you how and when to say thank you, your parents also unknowingly armed you with a powerful foundational networking tool for expressing altruism.

Consider any time that someone took the time to express her appreciation to you, how did you feel? Although you may describe it differently, knowing that someone appreciates you for whatever reason likely makes you feel great.

Therefore, if someone can make you feel great by saying thanks, then you can do the same for someone else. Moreover, if you have the power to make someone feel as great as you do when someone expresses gratitude to you, then thanking someone is a form of giving.

Knowing that just taking the time to say thank you is a means of giving, you should never be at a loss for ways to be altruistic. Moreover, you should go out of your way to find reasons to express your gratitude. This means identifying situations that are more than just saying thank you in an almost habitual manner, such as when someone holds the door for you. These are situations in which you can pour your heart into a big "thank you" and give the recipient that great feeling of exhilaration.

Additionally, when you thank someone, your words of praise, notes of thanks, or gifts of appreciation further etch you in their mind. You may never be able to make yourself indelible in the memory of your network. It is, however, this contact – no matter how trivial – that serves to create, strengthen and consummate your relationships, especially when regular contacts might be few and far between.

Saying thank you or expressing gratitude is more than just the right thing to do. Through gestures of appreciation, you serve to advance the altruistic aspect of your foundational networking.

Foundational Networking Exercise

For an entire week, focus on using words of appreciation (such as thanks or thank you) in a meaningful way in every e-mail which you send or respond to. Then challenge yourself to do it for an entire month. Then endeavor to make it a permanent practice.

Attention

"A good listener is not only popular everywhere, but after a while he or she knows something."
— Wilson Mizner

God gave us two ears and one mouth. God's reason for doing this was simply to remind us that we should communicate in the same proportion of these features: Listen twice as much as we talk.

However, listening is not just the act of not talking in a conversation. True listening is an active process whereby you give the other person your complete attention. You comprehend what he is saying. You seek clarification for what you do not understand. Depending on the subject, you are eager to learn more.

How do you feel toward the person who gives you his full attention? You feel as if you know him or at least you are very interested in knowing him. You cannot help but feel intrigued by someone so interested in you. As he has taken an interest in you, you certainly like him. Finally, you find yourself either trusting him or wanting to trust him.

Equally important, how do you feel about yourself when someone affords you this sort of attention? You feel important and special. You feel as if there is some sort of significance to you in the eyes of another. No doubt, this euphoria carries over into your demeanor. This person's interest in you has given you a sort of confidence.

When you commit to giving others this same attention, you become altruistic. You provide them your time and also bestow upon them an improved sense about themselves. Knowing this, you serve your foundational networking well if you adopt a genuine attitude of being interested in others and develop the habits of engaging them in conversation and learning about them.

Foundational Networking Exercise

Here is a checklist of actions that you should take before, during and after your encounters with others to ensure that you are affording them that appropriate attention.

Before

Recall: Reflect on conversations where someone has successfully engaged you in conversation. Reminisce on how she kept you engaged and demonstrated to you how she was truly interested in what you had to say.

Knowledge: Keep yourself reasonably educated on a broad array of current events, local news and general business activities. This will aid you in understanding as well as help you build follow-up questions.

Preparation: Play through in your mind a variety of scenarios as to how you might engage someone in conversation and keep her talking.

During

Body Language: Be sure to face the person and focus on him. Nod your head and politely remark to demonstrate you are listening to him (e.g., "I see," "okay" or "ahh").

Comprehend & Clarify: Focus on what the person is saying, and ensure that you understand it. If there is something you do not understand, do not gloss over it – ask for clarification.

Reiterate: Periodically, recap what the person has said so that you demonstrate your comprehension of what he is saying (e.g., "It sounds like a bad stint in corporate America led you to self-employment").

Delve Deeper: If appropriate, ask a follow-up question (or questions) that will allow you to better understand the person as well as demonstrate your continued interest in him (e.g., "Now I understand how you became self-employed, but how did you achieve such rapid growth?).

After

Remember: A conversation where you devote meaningful attention to another person becomes meaningless unless you undertake the activities that will help you to remember the particulars of the conversation. Do what you need to do to remember the important things about what the person said.

Follow Up: When you devote meaningful attention to another, you reinforce that altruistic act by following the conversation with a hand-written note, e-mail or telephone call where you mention something you have learned about the person.

Re-Use: As you encounter this person again (or connect him to others) draw upon what you know about him to further the relationship.

Gracious Receipt

"I have come to believe that giving and receiving
are really the same. Giving and receiving –
not giving and taking."
– Joyce Grenfell

The saying, "it is better to give than to receive" is true. It is true not because giving is the right thing to do but because there is truly more joy in giving to someone than receiving from them.

Think about it. Some of the greatest joys of parenthood are birthdays and holidays. Parents get so much satisfaction out of watching their excited children open gifts (which are usually toys that the kids will either ignore or break by day's end). While the parents are giving the gifts, they are the ones truly taking in the joy.

The same is true of a significant other to whom you bestow a meaningful gift. They get the present. You, however, get from them an indescribable delight in watching their reaction.

Giving to others is wonderful and that is why they say, "It is better to give than to receive."

However, as you involve yourself in your network, you cannot be (and do not want to be) always on the giving end. If you are out there truly networking, others will also give to you. They will give you referrals and other connections. They will share thoughts and ideas. They will contribute to you in every way that you would contribute to them. This is part of the mutual aspect of networking.

In networking, your attitudes and habits should be primarily focused on contributing to others, but it does not mean that you have somehow corrupted your foundational networking if someone else decides to contribute to your life. Eventually, you will (and should) receive.

There is nothing wrong if others seek to do things for you (give you gifts, provide you with referrals or even just lift your spirits). In fact, even in these moments you have an opportunity to advance yourself from a foundational networking perspective.

As much as people enjoy those things that you contribute to their lives, they want to give back to you as well. By opening yourself to the contributions of others and by graciously accepting them, you offer them the gift of receiving. The gift of receiving is simply giving others the opportunity to feel the joy of helping you.

Therefore, as you interact with others and attempt to identify ways to contribute to their lives, do not be afraid to share with them ways in which they can reciprocate. You should have the courage to ask for help when you need it. Adopt an attitude that makes you open to the encouragement and compliments of others. Get into the habit of sharing with those around you a sense of what types of referrals you want and people you seek to meet.

Along with giving to your network, you will open yourself to receiving from your network as well. At the same time, you give to others the joy of helping you. Thus, this makes the gift of receiving a very real part of altruism and foundational networking.

Foundational Networking Extra
Leather Work Gloves

From time to time, usually in a fit of frustration, my brother or sister will bark out to me "you are just like Dad." While in these moments my siblings do not necessarily mean this comment as a compliment, my father has generally coached me after the fact to respond with a "thank you."

With some of the comparisons, I certainly take issue. However, there is one I know to be absolutely true. My father is a difficult person to buy a gift for – in that respect I have, no doubt, become my father.

Every December, for as long as I can remember, I have struggled with finding my father a suitable Christmas present. My wife indicates the same thing about me.

She starts to fire up the question "What do you want for Christmas?" just after Thanksgiving and it never really gets answered. Then several weeks before my birthday, she is frustrated again.

As near as I can gather, there are a couple reasons for this. First, I do not see myself as a particularly extravagant person. Second, as for those things I do want or need, I do not make a production about them – I just go get them myself.

Is this a character flaw? We all have character flaws and maybe this is one of mine. I can accept that, as there are worse flaws to have. That being said, however, I can see how my reluctance to empower others to give to me has impaired my altruism.

A few years ago, this realization became very clear. It was Christmas Day. As my wife and I carefully distributed presents into neat little piles for our three eager kids, my daughter then proudly walked over to me with a gift, wrapped as only a 7-year-old could. With a big smile she said, "Here, Dad" and put it on my pile.

A few anxious minutes later we were ready to open presents. When it came my turn to open a present, immediately my daughter was encouraging me. "Dad, open that one," Logan excitedly said as she pointed to the present she had handed me.

As no one else was lobbying for me to do otherwise, I complied. Under the wrapping paper was a nice pair of leather work gloves – a good set for doing the work around the house I like to do. Logan was beaming ear-to-ear.

Before I could try them on she asked, "What do you think, Dad? Do you like them?"

I tried them on and said, "These are really great. I can really use these. Thank you. In fact, I have some work to do this week around the house and I will use them." Logan just smiled and smiled as we continued to open presents.

True to my word, a couple days later I started on a project of some sort in our house. And true to my word, I wore the leather work gloves. After I began, Logan came through where I was working. "Hey, Dad," she said, likely startling me over the sound of a power tool or the beating of a hammer, "how are the gloves?" She started to beam the same smile as the day I opened the present.

"Great. Thanks," I replied and returned to work. She asked me the same question once or twice more that day. Then on other occasions when she saw me wearing the gloves she would inquire again. Each time she was smiling away.

I realized that Logan got more joy out of giving these gloves to me than I had in receiving them. Do not get me wrong. These were nice gloves. They were better gloves than I would have bought for myself. It was a special gift considering who gave them to me. Nevertheless, they were just work gloves. If I used them like Logan wanted me to, the gloves would wear out.

However, to Logan, while the gift itself was not special, the giving of it was. She was able to experience the sheer joy of giving something at the holidays beyond what one might be scripted to do by one's first-grade teacher.

Stemming from this experience, I have resolved to be more open to empowering others to help me. I will endeavor to ask for help from others when I need it. Additionally, I will make an effort to let others know what things can benefit me.

I will do these things, not in an effort to get more (although that naturally occurs). Rather, I will do these things as a means of giving. Through the actions of my daughter, I recognize that by empowering others to help me I can give them joy and satisfaction by allowing them to give.

This holds true at home as well. On the refrigerator is a list of items that I can use to answer my wife's annual inquiry: "What do you want for Christmas?" I am still someone with simple needs and wants and I generally get something for myself when I need it. So, this list is nothing major. It is comprised of small, inexpensive items such as DVDs, books or minor tools. Nevertheless, I keep this list and add to it occasionally simply to enhance myself with respect to the gift of receiving.

And on that list, it is clearly written "Leather Work Gloves." Logan, the last pair wore out.

Thoughtfulness

"It's not the size of your shape or the shape of your size, but what's in your heart that deserves first prize."
— Andy Mills & Becky Osborn,
Co-Authors, Shapesville

Everything has a beginning to it. The giant oak tree starts as a tiny acorn. The mighty Nile River starts as an assortment of tiny streams. Any friendship you have ever enjoyed started with an initial introduction to or meeting with someone with whom you have common interests or convictions.

Knowing this, it begs the question, "What are the seeds of our altruism?" Where does it begin? Where do you get your inspiration or stimulation to reach out and provide assistance to others?

Is this trait an innate, instinctive behavior? That is, have forces akin to Darwin's theories of natural selection passed on to surviving generations the will to help those around them as a means of self-preservation?

Alternatively, is this something that your parents (along with teachers) instilled in you shortly after you learned to walk and talk? Are these actions of giving simply an extension of daily lessons on sharing and model citizenship for our formative years?

On the other hand, is your altruistic motivation an attribute that you develop naturally through successful interaction with others? In other words, does a series of prior trial-and-error experiences shape and direct your current acts of selflessness?

What is the true origin of giving? There are certainly many questions and where there are questions there is likely debate. The most accurate answer is complicated and you can probably describe it as being "all of the above."

If you are in business for yourself or you are career-minded and looking to advance yourself, you quite possibly have become a student of networking, meaning that you want to understand how this networking thing really works. You observe the successes (and failures) of others, looking to find patterns that you can replicate. You scour the Internet looking for every kernel of knowledge on the subject. In addition, you dissect and analyze every related book and article you can find – including this book.

Even if you are not that obsessed with learning about networking and using it in your business or professional life, you have likely uncovered a consistent message. While people may phrase this message in different ways and call it various things, the underlying theme of the message is the same: "If you want to get things from those in your network, you need to resolve to give to them first."

This is an important message. Quite simply, if you are not committed to giving to your network in some form or fashion, then you cannot expect to get anything either. Much like a bank account, you cannot make a withdrawal if you never make a deposit.

Now if, as part of your strategy to achieve greater success, you focus on giving so you will eventually get from your network, this is great. However, the fact of the matter is that if this is the only reason you are giving, then you are only halfway home. For you to take it the distance and totally surrender to the notion that "givers get," you need to give for no other reason than it is the right thing to do.

This is the starting point, the seeds of altruism. This is simply the act of focusing on ways in which you can be considerate of the feelings of others (whether you know them or not) and finding ways you can have a positive impact on their lives. This serves as your inspiration or stimulation to reach out and provide assistance to others. This mindset or attitude can be simply described as "thoughtfulness."

In his book, *Winning Without Intimidation*, Bob Burg discusses the fine art of thoughtfulness. Burg indicates that although it does not necessarily come naturally, being thoughtful is a simple idea that requires no incredible skill. It simply requires that we are considerate of others and we attempt to identify ways to improve their lives.

Drawing on a story by William A. Ward in the book *The Best Of Bits & Pieces*, Burg maintains that being thoughtful is nothing more than a habit. It encompasses such occasional and basic acts as holding a door open for someone or parking a bit farther from the entrance to leave the closer spaces for those who cannot get around as easily.

Answering the question I asked earlier, the seeds of altruism are nothing more than thinking about others. Thinking with respect to everyone you meet, "How can I add a little extra happiness to this person's life?" Thinking with respect to every situation you come upon, "How can I make this situation better in some way?" Then when you happen upon answers to these questions – even if it is only holding a door open – commit to action. If you focus on being thoughtful toward others and then acting upon it, eventually your thoughtfulness becomes a habit.

Burg indicates that others may or may not notice these acts of thoughtfulness. However, as he also indicates, it does not matter. What is important is that you continue to sow these seeds of altruism. If nothing else, your thoughts and deeds will make you feel better about yourself, which will then show up in your attitudes and habits.

At this point, you have arrived. You have embraced the true meaning of the phrase "if you want to get things from those in your network, you need to resolve to give to them first." You are giving not just to get – although that is a wonderful byproduct. You are giving because it is the right thing to do.

Foundational Networking Extra
Random Acts of Kindness

In July 1997, Doug Hull was walking with a friend on the Portage Canal, which divides Houghton from Hancock in the Upper Peninsula of Michigan. During his walk, he came upon a small bottle that looked like a saltshaker that had washed up on shore. Although it did not look like much, he picked it up. Upon closer inspection, he discovered that there was a message in the bottle.

The message was just a little communiqué offering well wishes and randomly intended for the person who found it. Doug had the good fortune of being on the receiving end. Thus, Doug thought that he might like to tell people about the wonderful message that he had found and the Internet seemed the perfect place to share such a story.

He had hoped that somebody had already created a web page that would be suitable for sharing his tale of this random act of kindness. He searched, but found none. Since Doug's philosophy about the Internet was that if you are trying to find a website on a certain subject and you cannot, it is somehow your duty to create one, he started what would become the Random Acts of Kindness web page (www.noogenesis.com/malama/kindness/) – which is sort of a random act of kindness in and of itself.

Like most, Doug became a busy person. His undergraduate work at Michigan Technological University led him to travels abroad to Oulu, Finland. From there, he started graduate work at Carnegie Mellon University in Pittsburgh. And finally, like any intelligent person, he capped a good education with a job in the real world. As such, he did not have the time to maintain this site in the manner he felt it deserved. Thus, he began looking for someone to adopt the site.

Then, in May 1999, while doing a search on "kindness," Duen Hsi Yen came across Doug's website and he was immediately captivated by the concept behind it. Duen forwarded Doug an e-mail expressing an interest in adopting the site. After a brief interview process – as Doug did not want to surrender the site he started to just anyone – Duen adopted the site.

On the site, Duen invites visitors to become writers and submit their own tales depicting random acts of kindness. Also in his instruction, Duen invites anyone to print out stories to share, such as:

A Christmas Gift: "I was given 4 Minnesota Timberwolves tickets as a Christmas gift. When I got home I found out that my wife had made plans with another couple. I called a few friends to see if they might want to go to the game, but no one was home. I then walked next door and made a deal with the neighbor kid. I would give him $120 worth of tickets if he promised to shovel my other neighbor's walk all winter. The other neighbor is an older retired gentleman, about 75, whose wife was just put in a nursing home. I feel good about being able to help someone with the tickets. The next door neighbor kid feels like he lucked out. And the old man received a random act of kindness."

Quilted Jacket: "I take a quilting class with some older women. I am the youngest at 44 years old. The oldest member, Liz, is in her 80s, widowed and on a set income. She had mentioned that she would like to make a project she had seen at the local fabric store, a quilted jacket, but the supplies were just too much for her to afford on her social security income. That day I went to the store and purchased a gift certificate for the amount it would take to purchase the supplies for the jacket and had it mailed to her anonymously. She was thrilled and overwhelmed that someone thought so much of her to do that! And it made me feel good, too!"

A Shoelace: "Giant Eagle is a large supermarket chain here in Pittsburgh and to their high credit they have a policy of hiring the learning disabled. At the high season of Christmas and Hanukkah the tension was dense at the check-out lines and one young chap was busy bagging produce that piled up in ever increasing amounts at the end of the conveyor belt. As busy as he was, he happened to have caught sight of his shoelace being untied. This threw the lad into some distress and he began to unravel his composure as he continued to bag the groceries. It was at this moment that a huge, burly policeman quietly left his security post and knelt down at the lad's feet and tied his shoelace for him. The radiance that fired to the face of the lad was a joy to behold as he too found a couple of seconds in the dexterity of his bagging to pat the head of our compassionate policeman."

True Bigheartedness

*"Generosity with strings
is not generosity; it is a deal."*
— Marya Mannes

Academic scholars define networking as "short-term altruism, long-term self-interest." In plain English, this means that your acts of generosity in the interim should be without any expectation of getting anything in return. However, eventually you need to anticipate that your networking efforts will generate some sort of return.

While conceptually this is relatively easy to comprehend, the practical application of this definition is a bit more problematic. The short-term portion of the definition – giving without expectation – is understandable. You should be doing things for others without being concerned as to what they will do for you in return.

However, the long-term portion of the definition – eventually you should anticipate a return – is not so clear. When does the short term, where you have no expectations, give way to the long term, where you can be hopeful of some sort of remuneration? A week? A month? A year? Longer?

In addition to when you can start to anticipate a return, what can you expect? Something commensurate with your overall contributions, however that might be measured? Is the remuneration something akin to an investment where the payback has some sort of compounded growth over what you gave? Or is there absolutely no perceptible correlation between what you give and what you get?

In reality, what you get and when you might get it is completely unknown. While you may not expect them to, some acts of generosity never come back to you. Some provide you an almost immediate return. Some offer remunerations when you least expect them.

For those times when you receive a return for your generosity, sometimes it seems that the return is substantial. Sometimes the return seems comparable to the effort you expended. Sometimes it seems minimal at best.

In reality, there is no rhyme or reason as to when or how much your generosity returns to you. The generosity of doing for others that underlies your foundational networking efforts is truly a leap of faith. In essence, you need to operate as if the short term is perpetual and the long term never arrives. Thus, by no means should you ever anticipate or expect a return from your networking.

Despite this, you are only human and thus you do. You have limited resources and time. Although you may not admit it, whenever you encounter an opportunity to contribute to your network, your brain undergoes a complicated analysis of whether you are using your resources and time effectively.

While this personal examination is only a matter of human nature, you need to remember that we are all connected. Your life has a connection to those you love and those you deeply respect as much as your life has a connection to those you do not care for.

The triumphs of others are, in effect, your gains too – perhaps not immediately, but certainly eventually. Likewise, the problems of others – even if those issues do not directly impact you – are your tribulations sooner or later.

For example, imagine if a longtime employee comes to you looking for assistance in finding local employment for his recently downsized spouse. If your reaction is to think, "Of what concern is this to me?" you will likely do nothing.

Eventually, not able to find employment nearby, the spouse of the employee must take a position out of state. Although disappointed, the employee must resign his position with your company and relocate. Not a problem, you think – you will just hire or promote someone else. That is what you do, thinking that business will just proceed as usual.

However, the employee who left had a considerable base of knowledge with respect to the particular part of your business he served. The new person will take years to achieve that intellectual capital. As a result, this particular part of your business does not work as effectively as it once did. This situation results in inefficiencies, cost overruns and strained relations with other departments within the business.

The person replacing the departing employee does not have the same management style. Employees within the department are less fulfilled. Some are not as committed to their responsibilities. Others begin to leave for new opportunities elsewhere. The discontentment and turnover further affects your business' overall performance.

While the departure of one employee may not destroy your business, it likely could have a serious impact. What is certain is that you could have avoided all this. All it would have required was for you to take an interest in your employee. Perhaps if you made a couple introductions on behalf of the employee's spouse. Perhaps if you simply passed on the spouse's resume. The effort would have been small. The cost of not making the effort is substantial.

As such, even if you can sense no logical benefit from your act of altruism (whatever it might be) it is best to do what you can to contribute to the accomplishments of others. Their new heights will serve to take you higher somehow.

Likewise, you are prudent to help others through whatever trials are confronting them, even if their trials seem to have no tangential relationship to your well-being. By doing so, not only will you be helping them to avoid pain, your actions may well serve to spare you too.

Similarly, the next time you find yourself dismissing the problem of another as "not concerning you," remind yourself that everyone is a vital thread in the tapestry of success. Everyone is connected. When one person succeeds, eventually everyone profits. When one person fails, we all suffer.

Thus, you need to get out there and help whomever you can, whether or not you see a benefit accruing to you. Somehow, some way, your actions will come back to benefit you.

Foundational Networking Extra
The Mousetrap

A mouse looked through the crack in the wall to see the farmer and his wife open a package. "What food might this contain?" He was devastated to discover it was a mousetrap.

Retreating to the farmyard, the mouse proclaimed the warning. "There is a mousetrap in the house! There is a mousetrap in the house!"

The chicken clucked and scratched, raised her head and said, "Mr. Mouse, I can tell this is a grave concern to you, but it is of no consequence to me. I cannot be bothered by it."

The mouse turned to the pig and told him, "There is a mousetrap in the house."

The pig sympathized, but said, "I am so very sorry, Mr. Mouse, but there is nothing I can do about it but pray. Be assured you are in my prayers."

The mouse turned to the cow. She said, "Wow, Mr. Mouse. I'm sorry for you, but it's no skin off my nose."

So, the mouse returned to the house, head down and dejected, to face the farmer's mousetrap alone.

That very night a sound was heard throughout the house – like the sound of a mousetrap catching its prey.
The farmer's wife rushed to see what was caught. In the darkness, she did not see it was a venomous snake whose tail the trap had caught.

The snake bit the farmer's wife. The farmer rushed her to the hospital, and she returned home with a fever. Everyone knows you treat a fever with fresh chicken soup, so the farmer took his hatchet to the farmyard for the soup's main ingredient.

But his wife's sickness continued, so friends and neighbors came to sit with her around the clock. To feed them, the farmer butchered the pig.

The farmer's wife did not get well. Eventually, she died. So many people came for her funeral, the farmer had the cow slaughtered to provide enough meat for all of them.

Personal Introductions

"The opportunity for brotherhood presents itself every time you meet a human being."
— Jane Wyman

When someone mentions the notion of altruism, generosity or giving to others, you probably wonder to yourself, "What do I have to offer?" You ponder how much money you have in your bank accounts. On the other hand, you may be unsure about what specialized information or skill you might have. Then again, you may question how much influence you can apply to a particular situation.

However, no matter how financially unfortunate, professionally inexperienced, or influentially insignificant you might be, you can still be altruistic. You have much to offer if you adopt an attitude of being committed to meeting new people and then develop the habit of connecting those people to ones you already know.

Take a moment and think about all the people you know. You have contacts from high school and college. You have contacts from your professional life – clients, co-workers, colleagues, vendors, and employees. You have relatives, in-laws, and family friends. You have those you know from church or other community involvement. You have those who you meet as result of your children. You know an incredible amount of people and that number, if you are engaged in any networking at all, is likely growing.

How many of these people know each other? As each of these factions represents a different segment of your life, it is likely that very few know one another.

How many of these people you know would benefit from you introducing them to someone else? Generally, nothing but good comes from meeting new people. Thus, everyone you know would benefit from your introductions. If you have a tremendous network of contacts and are willing to share them, you attract others to you. This is for two reasons. First, by having many contacts, people naturally conclude that others consider you worth knowing, likable and trustworthy and thus say to themselves, "if others know, like and trust her, then so should I."

Second, there is tremendous value in all the people you know. When you are willing to introduce those people to one another, you share that value. For that reason, these introductions in and of themselves are acts of altruism and others want to become involved with that selflessness.

Foundational Networking Exercise

Identify five individuals in your network. Then indicate the name of someone else in your network who you should introduce them to.

1. Introduce _____ to _____

2. Introduce _____ to _____

3. Introduce _____ to _____

4. Introduce _____ to _____

Foundational Networking Extra
The Baldzicki Factor

When you think of people who are best able to be altruistic, you are somewhat conditioned to focus only on certain types of individuals. You might picture a successful businessperson, a corporate executive or enterprising entrepreneur – each with a significant base of assets. You might imagine a government leader or high-ranking public official – each with a considerable degree of influence. You might conjure up images of scholarly or intellectual types – each possessing a highly specialized expertise or skill.

These are all reasonable choices of potentially altruistic people. Although they represent a diverse group of potential candidates, each has something desirable that they could potentially provide to others. Thus, they are in a strong position to be altruistic.

What about the "college dropout" – did you visualize that person? What about the person who is a laborer or a police officer – did you have an individual like this on your radar? What about the sales representative who has gone through six different jobs in three different industries in four years – did you imagine that this person would be the one to expand your network?

None of these are likely candidates you would consider to be in a position to be altruistic, are they? Before you fully commit to that line of thinking, however, consider the case of Steve Baldzicki.

Steve Baldzicki grew up in Mentor, Ohio – a community on the shores of Lake Erie about 30 minutes east of Cleveland. After graduating from Mentor High School, he enrolled at Mercyhurst College in Erie, Pennsylvania.

After two years, however, he dropped out of college and took a job for a short while in a lumberyard building pallets and boxes for General Electric. After his stint in hard labor, he became a police officer in Erie and then moved up to doing S.W.A.T. work in East Cleveland, where his dad was Chief of Police.

After a couple years in law enforcement, he relocated to Columbus, Ohio for a fresh start. For six months, he worked for Limited Brands, parent company of Victoria's Secret and Bath & Body Works. Then he took a position as a Receiving and Release Coordinator for the Franklin County Juvenile Detention Center. However, this did not last long either.

He went from college student to laborer to law enforcement officer to retail worker to corrections officer in a relatively short time. He had saved no money and he did not have any real expertise. He figured that his best bet for establishing himself would be in sales.

Steve began his sales career selling pagers. While he was relatively successful, with the explosion of cellular communication at the time, he was in a dying industry.

With his sales experience, he got a position selling commercial telecommunication products. Steve's timing was off again. Nationally, the telecommunication bubble was bursting. In six months time, he did not make a single sale and before he could resign, his employer completely closed its Ohio operations.

Steve Baldzicki does not sound like the person you long to meet. And, he certainly is not someone who is in a position to be considered altruistic. Nevertheless, he is.

Shortly after starting his career in the pager industry, Steve became extremely active in networking, both personally and professionally. In addition to becoming involved with AmSpirit Business Connections (serving as an Area Director for three years), he was active in several other organizations. Steve immersed himself in not just meeting others, but introducing those people to each other.

One month, on his own initiative, he decided to invite several of those he knew to a bar for a social gathering. More than 20 people attended. Everyone met someone new.

People encouraged Steve to do it again. So, he did. The next month he planned another social gathering. In preparation, he told those who attended the month before and asked them to spread the word among those they knew. This time, more than 50 people attended.

This went on for a few months and the number of attendees continued to grow. Before long, people were asking Steve if they could set up tables at his events to market their businesses. He agreed to do so for a small fee to cover costs.

With the small seed capital that these table fees generated for Steve, he invested in legal services to incorporate this business and establish a website to better promote his events. Dubbed Big Fish Networking, the networking events continued on a monthly basis. Over time, the number of attendees swelled to well over 500 people in some months.

During the rise of Big Fish Networking, Steve met many people, one of whom gave him an opportunity to do marketing for his title insurance company. This appeared to be his calling. Steve did so well marketing title and closing services that within two years' time a second title company came along and offered him a deal that he could not refuse. Two years later, a third title company came along and offered him an even better deal.

While enjoying this professional success, Steve Baldzicki has continued to build Big Fish Networking into Central Ohio's premier social networking events. Since the events began, Steve has been committed to making the Big Fish Networking events free for attendees and only asking vendors to pay a fee to exhibit.

These efforts led Steve to be named Entrepreneur of the Month for Columbus' *Business First* publication in April 2003. In addition, on several occasions various publications have written about Steve for his efforts with Big Fish Networking.

Also, because of the success of Big Fish Networking, Steve has been asked to partner his events with well known organizations such as the Greater Columbus Chamber of Commerce. And Big Fish Networking events have been held at Nationwide Arena, home of the National Hockey League's Columbus Blue Jackets, the Columbus Crew Stadium, and at the Ohio State University before an exhibition game for the Cleveland Cavaliers.

Steve Baldzicki, like most of us, was just an ordinary person trying to catch a break, and, like some of us, he had relatively nothing to offer. The jobs he held provided him with no real opportunity to save money and therefore he had no real assets from which to contribute to others. As a college dropout with an extremely diverse work history, he had no specialized knowledge or skill that he could add to people around him. Moreover, Steve never moved beyond the first or second rung of any organizational ladder, so he was in no position to be able to apply influence to any situation.

On paper, Steve is not someone you would characterize as having the propensity to be altruistic. Nevertheless, he is, and he has done it without assets, extreme intellect or influence.

The primary value that Steve brings to his ever-growing network is that he knows lots and lots of people. His database contains more than 10,000 names with relatively current information.

In addition, he is not just willing to introduce those in his network to others. He is eager to do so. Whenever he can, he will connect the "wants" and the "needs" that he becomes aware of in his network.

Finally, he is committed to continuing to meet new and interesting people. Steve does not discriminate. Within reason, he will take the time to meet anyone and everyone. For this reason, people truly want to connect with him, which further fuels his network.

Steve has built an incredible network and from that a wonderful business and promising career. However, to get this all started, all he had to offer others were introductions.

Unsolicited Generosity

> "That's what I consider true generosity.
> You give your all, and yet you always feel
> as if it costs you nothing."
> – *Simone de Beauvoir*

Altruism is essential to effective foundational networking. However, altruism is not necessarily about "what you give." It is entirely about "the spirit that moves you to give." It is about creating joy in the heart of another because of your contributions, deeds or comments.

To that end, the greatest impact you can have through your altruism involves the things you do when no one expects them. In other words, you maximize the amount of altruistic joy you share when others do not know it is coming. For example:

- You strip all the romance out of buying flowers for a spouse or significant other if the only time you do it is when she has to ask you to do so.

- You completely undermine the genuineness of your compliments if the only time you give them is when someone asks you to do so.

- Your random acts of kindness become a whole lot less thoughtful if they are only somehow orchestrated events.

- Your words and deeds of thanks and appreciation ring hollow if someone needs to coerce you to give them.

- Your acts of volunteerism become nothing more than a form of "indentured servitude" if others compel you to serve.

There is no doubt that your altruism is at its best when the generosity you convey is done so without anyone having to solicit it. Think of this in terms of being tickled.

Science has established that your touch can tickle someone else. Science has also established that individuals cannot tickle themselves.

The reason for the difference, scientists have concluded, is that the human brain distinguishes between "expected" and "unexpected" sensations. Thus, when individuals attempt to tickle themselves, these are expected sensations and the brain will not allow the tickling sensation to occur.

Just as individuals cannot tickle themselves, you cannot convey true altruistic joy on others if they know it is coming or if they need to solicit it. Your altruism is most effective when you sneak up on others to present it.

Spouses or significant others are romantically moved when they are showered with cards and gifts when they least expects them. Your compliments have a special meaning when you give them without any sort of solicitation. Likewise, the referrals you give and the business contacts you create for others become extraordinary acts of altruism when you do them without any sort of prompting.

Therefore, truly embracing an altruistic attitude in furthering your foundational networking requires you to get out there and go tickle someone – metaphorically speaking of course.

Foundational Networking Exercise

Create a list of at least three acts of altruism that you could commit to performing that would come as a pleasant surprise to the recipient.

1. _____

2. _____

3. _____

Integrity

"Real integrity is doing the right thing,
knowing that nobody's going
to know whether you did it or not."
— Oprah Winfrey

The final vital aspect of foundational networking, the developing of know, like and trust with those around us, is through adopting attitudes and developing habits of integrity. Trust is simply a product of integrity.

This, of course, begs the question, what is integrity? There is no simple answer. It is comprised of many elements. Integrity, which relates to the Latin adjective *integer* meaning whole or complete, is comprised of honesty, character and accountability. Then each of those words is comprised of other attributes.

Integrity, in one sense, is a very simple matter. You know when you see it. Yet in another sense, the concept can be rather complicated. How do you describe it? The answer to that is not clear.

Integrity is perhaps the most vital aspect of foundational networking. You can maintain some semblance of a network without an iota of altruism. Moreover, completely lacking a positive presence, while detrimental, is not catastrophic to having a functioning network. However, without integrity you have nothing. People will simply not look beyond this particular deficiency.

Integrity has a variety of definitions, which all allude to similar concepts and depend on a host of factors, such as:

• Past experience with a person and with their friends;

• Opinions of the actions a person has taken; and,

• Rumor or influence by others' opinions.

This section will explore the components of integrity. As such, it will examine the various attitudes and habits that are (or are not) integrity.

While doing so, it is important to note that others do not measure your integrity based on major interactions or significant transactions. Rather, people look to how you perform on the smaller tests of integrity. Some examples might be:

- Are you the person who is willing to stand in a long line (whether you are happy about it or not) or are you the type seeking to connive your way closer to the front using your contacts or authority?

- Are you the person who will dutifully pay a late fee when you do not get a bill paid on time or are you the type to seek a waiver using excuses and threats?

- Are you the person who honorably points out a mathematical error when you are undercharged (or happen to overcharge a customer or client) or are you the person who accepts the benefit of the miscalculation?

People focus on the little things because no one fails on the big ones. Consider if someone were to entrust you with a reasonably large sum of money to hold in escrow or as a down payment on future services or purchase. You handle these monies in an appropriate manner.

Certainly, there are stories of business types (whether blue collar or professional) who have left town or failed to deliver in these situations. This does happen. These situations represent an incredibly small fraction of a percentage, however. For the most part, people exhibit the appropriate level of personal and professional integrity in these situations. These situations do not serve as the basis on which others judge your level of integrity.

Therefore, it is the little things that others use to gauge the extent of your integrity. Consider the short poetic fable by an unknown author titled *For Want Of A Nail*.

For want of a nail, the shoe was lost;

For want of a shoe, the horse was lost;

For want of the horse, the rider was lost;

For want of the rider, the battle was lost;

For want of the battle, the kingdom was lost;

And all for the want of a nail.

With respect to this section, the point or moral of this poetic fable is that the little things you do (or fail to do) serve to bolster or undermine how others perceive your integrity. It seldom comes in question when it relates to matters of great (or even medium) significance.

Consistent Comfort

> "(Many executives) will not enter into
> a relationship because they will not feel comfortable
> conducting business with someone they do not
> feel 100 percent comfortable with."
> *– Neil Payne*

Imagine that you walk into a business or social function. It is a strange setting in that you know no one.

Shortly after you enter, you encounter two people almost simultaneously, neither of whom you have met before. The first seems to shun you. He makes eye contact and appears to examine you from head to toe. Nevertheless, he says nothing and turns to walk away, not even affording you a smile.

The second person also makes eye contact. He, however, immediately breaks into a warm, welcoming smile. Before you can even smile back, this person has extended his hand and offered his name. Naturally, you respond. You smile, shake his hand and offer your name in return.

It does not stop there, however. This person engages you in light conversation, seizing upon perhaps something you are wearing, the weather or current events. He is not glad-handing you, but rather has engaged you in genuine conversation.

This does not last long, but before it is over the person has made you feel at ease. In addition, he has introduced you to someone else or directed you to the buffet or bar.

Throughout the event, you continue to encounter the first person. He remains unapproachable. You offer a slight smile, but that only serves to shorten any eye contact that he has with you. The mere sight of this person makes you feel uneasy.

Similarly, throughout the event, you continue to encounter the second person. Every time there is welcoming eye contact, a broad smile and more light conversation. This person feels like an old friend.

Without question, if you have a choice between associating with the first and the second person, you will select the second person. He has made you feel comfortable – you have a sense of knowing him, you cannot help but like him and you feel as if you can trust him.

While these may be extreme examples on the opposite ends of the spectrum, they do nevertheless underscore the point that you make assessments about other people's integrity even before you contemplate any business or financial transactions. Moreover, if you are making these determinations based on passing interactions, you can expect that others are doing the same of you.

How you make others feel through your interactions with them has a direct relationship to the level of integrity they determine you to have. You should know by now that a simple smile can brighten another's day. Further, there is little doubt that some words and actions can be positive and uplifting, while others can be corrosive and destructive.

In relating to others, you need to adopt the attitude that it is important that you consistently make them feel secure and at ease, as you would a guest in your home. Then it is important that you develop the habits to ensure this occurs. These simple actions will plant the seeds in the minds of others that you are a person of integrity.

Foundational Networking Exercise

What are seven things that you can do make others feel comfortable around you?

1. _____

2. _____

3. _____

4. _____

5. _____

6. _____

7. _____

Trusting Nature

"Trust men and they will be true to you; treat them greatly and they will show themselves great."
— Ralph Waldo Emerson

If you want to get things from your network, then you need to commit to giving to your network. If you want referrals, you need to give referrals. If you want information, you need to be willing to offer it. If you want encouragement from your network, you had better be giving encouragement.

This is true of every aspect of networking including trust. If you want others to trust you, you need to be trusting of them first.

Imagine interacting with someone who indicates in one way or another that he does not trust you. How does this make you feel? You are likely hurt and maybe even offended. You probably wonder how and why he has drawn this conclusion. In any respect, this person certainly has not endeared himself to you and thus you are not open to trusting him either.

Now, imagine interacting with someone who expresses that he trusts you either in word or in deed. How do you feel now? You likely feel a wave of warmth overcome you. This person's trust serves as an affirmation of all the good and honest things you have done. Most importantly, you cannot help but trust him in return.

With this, if you are looking for those in your network to trust you, you need to adopt the attitudes and develop the habits that allow you to trust them first.

This is not to suggest that you take unnecessary risks or place yourself in a precarious position in the name of gaining another's trust. You need to use common sense and your best judgment in offering your trust in pursuit of theirs. Nevertheless, you must trust others before they will consider trusting you.

Foundational Networking Extra
Here You Go, Partner

When I practiced law, Larry LeMasters was one of the best clients I could have ever hoped to represent. He is the founder and CEO of Mountaineer, Inc., a logistic and chemical distribution company he founded out of his garage in 1975. Since that time he has grown Mountaineer into a multi-million dollar enterprise that services suppliers to the automotive industry across the Midwest.

I became Larry's attorney and started providing services before we even met. At the time, he needed some assistance with a particularly specialized project. As I had skills that were beneficial for the project, another attorney referred him to me.

As this was my first project for Larry and because he had such an impressive business enterprise, I felt compelled to do everything with perfection. I read and re-read the report that I had drafted. I went to the office supply store and bought a special binder with which to present my work to Larry. I compiled a comprehensive invoice, detailing every moment I had spent on the project.

When I finished my work, I contacted Larry and arranged to meet him to go through what I had done. Larry asked that we meet at his house.

When I arrived on the day of our meeting, Larry was waiting for me in his driveway. He greeted me like an old friend and thanked me for meeting him at his home. He led me in through the garage, giving me the "nickel tour" of his house as we headed toward the kitchen. He politely directed me to a seat at his kitchen table and then offered me a soda, water or a beer.

As I went through the high points of my work, I got the sense that he was not interested in the "how's and the why's," but rather the results – "Can we do it?" Nevertheless, he was polite and permitted me to walk through my report step-by-step, with a bit of a tremble in my voice. Again, he was the client, and a new one at that. I wanted to present myself and the material perfectly.

When I finished talking, Larry immediately thanked me and glowed on and on about how I delivered exactly what he needed. He made me feel as if I provided real value to him. I felt a sense of accomplishment and relief – this project was complete and well received.

Then Larry asked me what he owed me. I went silent. Immediately, I felt a wave of anxiety and my sense of relief faded. In the field of professional services, there was always the risk that an invoice that did not meet the client's expectations could overshadow the perception of doing well on a project. I removed the carefully prepared invoice from my portfolio and handed it over to him with a slight tremble in my hand.

Larry quickly thumbed through the three pages of detail I had provided him. I could feel sweat rolling down my back. He set it down and immediately started in on me.

"Listen. You are now my attorney, so I trust you. I don't need an invoice. From now on just tell me what I owe. And, if you feel you need to give me something for tax purposes, then just hand me a page with a total on it and not all this detail."

I had no idea how to react. In a bewildered manner, I said, "Okay." Larry asked me what the total bill was. I told him, still nervous as to his reaction. Without saying a word, he then excused himself and went into the next room. I simply sat there, not knowing what to expect.

Within two minutes, Larry returned. In his hand, he had a check. He extended his hand and offered it to me. "Here you go, partner," he said (he seldom called me by name – Captain, Counselor, Rascal, Partner, Chief, or Buddy, but not usually Frank).

I uttered a somewhat stunned "Thank you." I looked at the check and was completely astonished – it was for the full amount. Although I had only been in private practice for a little over a year, I had seen a lot with respect to having clients pay my invoices. But I had very few who paid me on the spot, and I certainly never had a client pay me so quickly for so much. I could hardly contain myself.

My initial encounter with Larry was a fair representation of our entire professional relationship. He would ask me to take on an assignment. Whenever he did, I would make time for it. When I was finished, he would tell me how appreciative and impressed he was with my efforts. Then he would pay me, always telling me how much he trusted me and that he was happy that I was on his team.

My situation was not unique, though. As I got to know Larry better, I met the people around him. Larry surrounded himself with a legion of vendors, professionals and employees that he treated in a similar fashion – with respect and trust.

In return, they made Larry a priority, giving him their best effort. Most importantly, like me, everyone associated with Larry had great respect for and trust in him.

Role Recognition

"Success is sweetest when it's shared."
— Howard Schultz

It is human nature to seek challenges and overcome them. If you are honest with yourself, this is the substance of your dreams. Whether this relates to advancing in your career, growing a business or conquering your first marathon, you long to overcome a good challenge.

This is, in part, because everyone loves a winner. Not only does everyone love a winner, everyone wants to associate with one. People want to feel a part of the triumph and they want to feel as if, somehow, they contributed to it.

Ponder for a moment the various times when someone accomplished something great – whether it was you or someone else. In at least one of those situations, there was likely an individual who took some credit for the feat when he deserved little, if any at all.

How did you feel toward this person? Even if it was not your accomplishment, you probably felt a little cheated. Moreover, you likely questioned the person's motives and questioned the integrity of everything that he had ever been given credit for accomplishing. Whatever the case, you had little interest in associating with him and you likely preferred to distance yourself from him.

While each of you has been in situations where a piece of the glory has been hijacked, you have probably also been in the opposite position. Something wonderful occurs and the person solely or primarily responsible goes to great lengths to share the limelight with just about everyone.

As an example, the firm lands the major account and everyone applauds the person who spearheaded the effort. She then humbly deflects attention to others. "The people in marketing crafted the wording perfectly ... the graphics folks brought it to life ... the accountants really sharpened their pencils ... the staff accumulated timely and accurate information for the underlying report."

How did you feel about that person? You felt energized. You were appreciative of her sharing the accolades. You certainly trusted her and were more than willing to go to great lengths to ensure that there were more successes. If nothing else, you wanted to associate with her.

For purposes of foundational networking, which of these two individuals should you aspire to become? The answer is obvious. Become the person you aspire to network with.

The reality is that you do nothing alone. With everything you have or will ever achieve, credit is due to someone else. Therefore, no matter what milestone you attain, eagerly and energetically share credit with those deserving people around you.

A wonderful quote is, "It is amazing how much we can accomplish when it doesn't matter who gets the credit." It is wonderful for two reasons. The first is that no particular person is given credit for creating it. That is a fitting result, considering the quote. Someone originated the saying, but being true to his or her own guidance, he or she was not concerned with taking credit for it.

The second reason is that it alludes to the all too common practice of wasting a tremendous amount of time and energy to determine who should be anointed with the appropriate kudos on a particular achievement. At the same time, the quote should remind you that it does not matter whether or not you get any credit. All that really matters is that you focus on giving credit to whomever you can.

Foundational Networking Exercise

List five accomplishments or milestones that you have achieved. Then indicate at least two other people who deserve credit who you might not have otherwise considered.

1. _____

    a. _____

    b. _____

2. _____

    a. _____

    b. _____

3. _____

    a. _____

    b. _____

4. _____

    a. _____

    b. _____

5. _____

    a. _____

    b. _____

Reliability

"Ability without dependability has no value."
– Unknown

There is much that others can compliment you for. Others can commend you for your intellect or work ethic. They can praise you for your appearance or sense of style. Moreover, they can extol your manners or the compassion you exhibit toward others. You can hope for compliments from others for virtually every aspect of your life.

Nevertheless, despite the broad range of areas for which you can receive accolades, one aspect of your life deserves maximum attention in an effort to earn tribute from others: your reliability.

Whether or not you receive compliments for this, you need to ensure that you do whatever you can to be someone whom others can rely upon. Why? Reliability is the foundation upon which all your talents and characteristics rest. Much like in mathematics where zero times any other number equals zero, excellence in any aspect of your life is meaningless without reliability.

You can have a great work ethic – where you generally arrive early, happily put in long hours and tirelessly work to get the job done. You can be tremendously well organized – where you have a good handle on your resources, an understanding of what needs to be done when, and the ability to combine the two to effectively complete tasks. You can possess wonderful creativity – where you consistently come upon groundbreaking ideas and insightful thoughts.

However, none of this – work ethic, organizational skills or creativity – will get you anywhere unless you are reliable. This means, for starters, that you need to do what you say you are going to do. Moreover, you must be on time for appointments as well as consistently meet deadlines. Likewise, you should commit yourself to generating productive results as part of your efforts.

Reliability is everything, and it is important to note that whether you are reliable is entirely in your control. You (and you alone) control whether you do what you say you are going to do. You control whether you will be on time for appointments. You control whether you meet deadlines. You largely control whether you generate productive results. In short, you are reliable or you are not. There is very little, if any, middle ground.

Does reliability really matter to your overall integrity? Absolutely. Reliability goes to the heart of trust, which is vital to foundational networking.

In interacting with others, reliability needs to be your first and most important priority. It is, in essence, a contract with those around you. You say to those in your network, "In exchange for your reliance on me (however that manifests itself), I will do what I say I am going to do when I say I am going to do it."

This contract does not state, "I will do what I say I am going to do, unless I have an excuse otherwise." It does not state, "I will do what I say I am going to do, maybe." This portion of the agreement is an unconditional affirmation of what the other party should be able to expect. Period.

Despite this unconditional affirmation, there are those moments when external forces intervene. For example, there are situations when a computer network glitch occurs, significantly impairing your ability to complete a proposal in a timely fashion. In these situations, your reliability may potentially be subject to tainting.

However, this potential taint will not occur (or if it does it will not last for long in the mind of others) if you ensure three things:

1. **Standing**: You have solidly established yourself over time through past actions to be reliable. Following the above example, if you usually get proposals and projects done in a timely manner the countless other times someone has entrusted you, one infraction should not impair your overall image of reliability.

2. **Forewarning**: As soon as you know of the intervening external force, you alert the other person to minimize the impact of your failing (albeit beyond your control) on him or her. Again, following the above example, if the unforeseen computer glitch is causing you to miss the deadline or otherwise alter someone's expectations, as soon as you are aware of the problem you need to make every attempt to alert the person who is relying on you.

3. **Uncommon**: You need to ensure that these occurrences represent the rarest of exceptions and that these occasions are in no way an indication of any sort of pattern. Returning to the example, computer glitches do occur and they can thwart your ability to complete assignments on time (as can a half dozen other external forces). However, if you undertake the appropriate planning and precautions, these situations should be infrequent if not once in a lifetime. As computers are prone to glitches, reliability dictates that you simply employ a contingency factor into your plans, like getting the work done well in advance or having an alternative computing solution in place.

You might think or even ask, "How can I establish myself as being reliable if I have never been relied upon?" The simple answer is that whether you know it or acknowledge it, people are relying on you continually. And even if they do not rely on you directly, they observe you as others rely on you. Every day somebody is relying on you to be somewhere at an appointed time, even if it is only to pick up your kids from school. Right now, chances are someone is relying upon things that you have told them, such as "I will be there at 7:30 a.m. sharp." Moreover, each day someone is relying on a follow-up on something you have committed to, such as "I will call you sometime tomorrow afternoon."

Thus, over time, your reliability builds. Every time you arrive to a meeting on time, those around you deem you more reliable. Every time you do what you say you are going to do, your image takes on a greater and greater persona of reliability.

Unfortunately, reliability does not build at the same rate as it deteriorates. That is, an unreliable action or inaction will do more harm than a similar reliable action or inaction.

You need to adopt the attitude that being reliable is an all-or-nothing proposition – you are either reliable or you are not. Then, you need to approach everything you do with the sense that your perceived reliability is paramount to your success.

- If you tell someone you will meet her at 5:00, arrive at 4:50 so as to leave no doubt as to your planned presence.

- If you tell someone you will call, that is what you do.

- If you commit to deliver something by Friday, you do so on Thursday or Friday, at worst.

If someone tells you that you are smart, you should say thank you. If they say you are a hard worker, you nod in appreciation. If another indicates you are well mannered, you smile in gratitude. But if someone says he or she can depend on you, or if anyone calls you their "go to" person, or if an individual refers to your abilities or character as unfailing, then you do all three. Because when they do any of these they are indicating you are reliable, which is the highest compliment of all.

Foundational Networking Extra
For Want of a Donut

A couple years ago, I had breakfast with an AmSpirit Business Connections member. During the course of discussing various topics, this particular member indicated to me that she was no longer interested in referring business to another person in her chapter.

I thought it was a curious statement, especially since these two had been in the chapter for several years together and there had never been any hint of a problem. They exchanged referrals with one another. They were genuinely cordial with one another. They spoke highly of one another to others. Therefore, I probed. Why would this relationship falter all of a sudden?

It did not take long to uncover what had occurred, and what she indicated as her reasoning was enlightening. There was nothing major that this particular member had done. This particular member was clearly a competent professional. This particular member had never failed to service any of the referrals he received. This particular member said nothing to offend anyone. So, why would someone's feelings change regarding this particular member? A hint of the answer can be summed up in one word: Donuts.

The chapter to which these members belong has a system in which each member takes turns bringing breakfast items to share at the weekly meeting. Following a pre-set schedule, each member has responsibility to bring some sort of breakfast food to share with his or her fellow members for two consecutive weeks. Some members will bake cookies or coffee cake. Other members will purchase bagels or donuts to share.

When it was this particular member's turn to provide breakfast for the chapter, he simply did not do it. This particular member failed to bring breakfast not just one week but both weeks. This particular member did not have a minor oversight. He knew, as do all the members, well in advance when it was his turn. It was not a case of forgetting. The chapter members reminded him the week before and during the first week that he failed.

According to my conversation over breakfast, when this member was politely confronted with his failure each meeting, there was no contrition on his part. Rather, he responded with a smirk on his face in a manner that might indicate that he would not be bothered with such a trivial matter.

Now, admittedly I do not know the actual reason for this member's shortcoming. It may well have been an innocent oversight or there may have been a perfectly acceptable explanation. Whatever the actual reason or rationale did not matter. What did matter, however, was the perception of those around him.

Their perception was that the chapter entrusted him with a task and he failed to come through. Furthermore, and likely worse yet, he was not in the least bit remorseful about it.

On some level, this may seem petty. He really harmed no one, and, in fact, one could argue that he probably saved his fellow chapter members from unhealthy, unneeded calories.

On another level, this is not petty at all. True, he injured no one. However, he did violate the trust of those who relied on him.

Unfortunately, the person ultimately failed in business. While there are probably several reasons for the failure, an argument can be made that it happened all for the want of a donut.

Honesty

"Honesty is the first chapter in the book of wisdom."
– Thomas Jefferson

There is little question that honesty goes to the heart of integrity, which is integral to foundational networking. The issue with respect to honesty is that often life calls upon you to be truthful when few people (if anybody) will ever know that you have been. That is the nature of honesty.

It may be a time when you inadvertently overcharge a client for something, and no one would know the difference. It may be a time when your employer gives you a reimbursement and only you know that you are not entitled to it. Perhaps, it will be a time when someone praised you for something and someone else deserved the credit.

In this moment, your conscience reminds you, "Honesty is the best policy." Even if no one else knows, choose the path of sincerity, truthfulness and integrity versus one of disingenuousness, deceit and treachery. By doing so, you will be further ahead in the end.

Remember that the true foundational networking opportunity associated with honesty is not what you exhibit to others. The true value of honesty is what you demonstrate to yourself.

You can fudge on your resume a bit and no one may ever know. In the short run, this deceit may help you get the job, a promotion or higher salary.

In the end, what does this do to you? You derive less satisfaction from your achievements because you know you did not come by them honestly. Moreover, you are less confident in your abilities as they did not get you where you are. Finally, you are insecure with your position as you constantly wonder if others somehow will uncover your deceit.

More often than not, opportunities to be honest will be situations where only you will know the difference. Again, that is the nature of honesty. While temptation may lure you to dishonesty, it is overcoming the temptation that enhances the value of your honesty by giving you satisfaction and confidence in yourself.

Foundational Networking Extra
One Fore Honesty

In the fall of 2005, Adam Van Houten was a sophomore at Mount Gilead High School in Mount Gilead – a small town in north central Ohio. On October 14th and 15th, he was competing in the Ohio high school state golf championship, which was being held at the Firefox Golf Club, just south of Columbus.

After two days of play, Adam was in the clubhouse with a 7-stroke lead over all the other golfers who had finished. The Division II state championship was all but a certainty for him. In fact, there was only one person on the course who had a realistic chance of even tying Adam – forcing a play-off.

However, as Adam was waiting, something happened. On the official scoreboard was his name followed by the number 74 – his score for the second round of the state championship.

As he was mulling over his final round of golf, something did not seem right in his mind. Although he would have normally kept for his own record an unofficial tally of his score, the one he was keeping for this round of play was taken somewhere by a gust of wind on the first nine holes. Even without this tally, he felt that something was wrong with the posted score.

After quickly consulting with his coach and father on his own, he went to the Ohio High School Athletic Association officials and asked to check his scorecard. According to Ohio High School Golf Championship protocol, each player records the scores of his playing partner.

After the round is complete, each player checks the tally the other player kept, and, assuming it is correct, signs the card to indicate that it is accurate and authentic. Under OHSAA rules, each player is "responsible for the correctness of the score for each hole on his score card."

It did not take Adam long to discover what was troubling him. Although he had checked his card twice before signing it, on the 10th hole of his final round, his playing partner had entered a five for his score. He, along with help from his father, who followed his son shot by shot for the entire round, reviewed in his mind the details of the 10th hole. Although distraught, Adam clearly determined that his score for this hole should have been a six, instead of a five.

Adam quickly disclosed the error to the OHSAA officials. Thus, his final round should have been a 75 and not a 74, making his total 36-hole tournament score a 145 rather than a 144. As the next closest competitor posted a 151, Adam's score would have still been enough for the OHSAA to declare Adam the Division II champion. Because he had already signed his scorecard, however, OHSAA officials had no choice but to disqualify him, even though they were tickled by his honesty. Rather than being crowned state champion, Adam's name had a prominent "DQ" next to it on the scoreboard.

If Adam had kept quiet, no one would have known about the scorecard error. No one would have even suspected anything. Adam would have been the 2005 OHSAA Division II Boy's Golf Champion.

While Adam might have carried some guilt with him if he had not admitted the error that disqualified him, if we put that aside we know with a degree of certainty what types of awards and accolades a high school golf champion garners. The OHSAA would have given Adam a medal to hang around his neck and he would have gone down in the record book as state champion.

Further, everyone at the event would have congratulated him and held him in high esteem. We need to remember, however, that he would have had to share that spotlight with the champions from other divisions as well as the team champions.

Adam would have certainly been welcomed back at Mount Gilead High School as a conquering hero, as state championships do not happen often in most communities. This fanfare would not have lasted long, however, as the end of the Ohio High School Golf Championships coincides with the start of high school football playoffs and the start of basketball, wrestling and other sport seasons.

The community of Mount Gilead itself might erect a small sign on each major road leading into the limits announcing "Home Of Adam Van Houten, 2005 Ohio High School Division II State Golf Champion." This, however, would soon become just another sign that we pass and ignore as irrelevant.

Certainly, there would be an article in the paper about Adam's achievement. But the article would have appeared only in the local paper, *Morrow County Sentinel*. Moreover, the article would likely only be a few short paragraphs, as it would be competing with important local activities and other sporting events.

Adam did not win the Ohio High School Division II State Golf Championship. His character, honesty and courage would not allow it. Adam, and Adam alone, saw that the OHSAA had posted a 74 when he knew, somehow, that the score should have been 75. He alone took action to review his scorecard. He alone disclosed his error to OHSAA officials when he discovered it. What did this honesty gain him?

He did not get a medal from the OHSAA. However, the Mount Gilead Exempt Local School Board of Education officially recognized Adam for his achievement and sportsmanship and gave him a plaque declaring him "Our State Champion."

Although Adam did not stay at the OHSAA Golf Championships long enough to realize it, his honesty created an atmosphere of admiration. As he embarked upon his junior and senior year of high school golf, many of those whom he competed against (as well as their coaches and fans) greeted him with congratulations and those people hold Adam in high esteem. Moreover, he did not have to share that spotlight with anyone else.

Despite the disqualification, Adam was welcomed back at Mount Gilead High School as more than just a conquering hero. His friends and classmates were able to look beyond the technical disqualification and recognize that he was truly the best high school Division II golfer in Ohio. Beyond that, they acknowledged Adam for what he truly is: honest and courageous. This is something that they will always see in Adam no matter what sport is teeing up or kicking off.

While there may be no plans for a sign announcing Adam's championship achievement at the Mount Gilead Village limits, members of the community recognized him in other ways. A car dealership purchased a large space in the local paper. In the space was a picture of Adam along with the words "In Ohio – Integrity Has A New Spelling. It is spelled: Adam Van Houten."

Deb Clauss, Mount Gilead High School principal, will tell anyone who asks, "Yes, this young man is one of my students. The story is correct – and we are very proud of the actions of this young man. … He is a great example of integrity and ethics in sports!"

As you might guess, there was an article in the paper about Adam's honesty. There was a rather lengthy article in the *Morrow County Sentinel*. There was also another one in the *Mansfield News Journal*. Moreover, there was another one in the *Columbus Dispatch* by sports columnist Bob Hunter. Normally devoting time to remarking about the Ohio State Buckeyes, Columbus Blue Jackets or professionals sports teams from Cleveland and Cincinnati, Hunter wrote of Adam:

"How do you measure a champion? By scores or by sportsmanship? By hardware or by honor? By medals or by principle? Adam Van Houten is not a state golf champion. He doesn't have the hardware or the medals, doesn't have the title or the line in the record book. But Van Houten … has integrity, and that's at least as important."

Clearly, the awards and accolades of honesty have proved far more beneficial to Adam than those of a state high school golf championship. However, this same lesson holds true for everyone.

On October 15, 2005, Adam Van Houten started the second round of the Ohio State High School Golf Championships. On that day, his intention was simple – to win the OHSAA Division II state golf championship. If you check the record book, officially it did not happen.

On that day, Adam did not intend to become an icon for honesty, values and courage in high school athletics and in a small Ohio community. Fate, however, intervened and he did.

On that day, what Adam did do, whether he realizes it or not, was perform an important experiment. Somewhere on the 10th hole of Foxfire Golf Course during the 2005 OHSAA Division II Golf Championship, someone made what amounted to nothing more than a clerical error. A couple hours later, Adam complicated that mistake with his own minor oversight. These two elements set the stage to test the cliché "honesty is the best policy."

Acts of Contrition

"True repentance means making amends with
the person when at all possible."
– *Lawana Blackwell*

We are all human. We are all brought to this world in the same way. We all have the same basic needs and desires. And we all have a propensity toward imperfection.

As such, you have made mistakes and you will make mistakes. This is part of life. This is part of being human.

Certainly there are times when your faults affect no one but yourself and then there are other times when your actions (or failure to act) harm others. It might be that you hurt someone's feelings. You might cause damage to someone's person, property or reputation. You could let down those who rely on you. Whatever the case, the consequences of your failure are not restricted to you.

Even though you diligently work to minimize these shortcomings, when they occur, you should never be too proud to say, "I am sorry."

Consider the person you know who can never find the courage to have contrition. The person may boldly maintain, "I am not going to apologize!" Whatever his reason for not apologizing, how do you feel toward this person? He does not impress you. He may stir up a sense of anger in you. He tends to make you feel more uncomfortable and less trusting around him.

Contrast that with the person who freely admits when she has done something wrong and then offers a genuine apology. The person may say in a conciliatory manner, "I am really sorry for what I did." How do you feel about this person? She gives you a cause for reflection. She immediately diminishes (if not completely disarms) any anger you might have. She becomes someone with whom you can feel a sense of security.

Unfortunately, companies and individuals habitually resist admitting fault or expressing regret to anyone. There are a couple reasons for this. Some point to an American culture that dubs contrition as a sign of weakness. Others point to the fear of lawsuits or possible harm to business or career for owning up to even the smallest mistakes.

Neither of these is true, however. If you have contrition, you build better relationships. As for being a sign of weakness, consider how much courage it takes for you to face a client, friend or employee and say, "I am truly sorry." It is not an easy thing to do. As such, a genuine act of contrition serves to demonstrate your strength and self-confidence and does nothing to expose you as being weak.

If that is not a convincing argument, consider the last time someone offered you a genuine act of contrition for whatever reason. What was your impression of him? You likely did not perceive him to be weak. Rather, he moved you to feel compassion for him. In the end, you felt closer to and more trusting of him through his expression of contrition.

A genuine act of contrition will do that for you as well. Therefore, always be open to saying, "I am sorry." Just speaking these words might not right the wrong or repair the damage to another. Nevertheless, an apology is always the first step in a genuine act of contrition.

You need to remember that in establishing a genuine act of contrition there is a tremendous difference between 'saying sorry' and 'being sorry.' Generally, an effective apology – a genuine act of contrition – includes four key ingredients:

1. **Sincere Repentance**: Every apology should start with a genuine and heartfelt, "I'm terribly sorry for the harm I have caused," or words to this effect. While an apology, no matter how motivated, might be the first step toward repentance, words alone will not create a genuine act of contrition. To achieve this, your words should be laced with genuine feelings of regret and remorse.

2. **Information**: In addition to sincere repentance, those who are wronged appreciate a clear, honest explanation as to how and why something went wrong. In short, you need to not only acknowledge the mistake, but also own up to your responsibility in the mistake occurring.

3. **Corrective Action**: After offering sincere regret and a reasonable explanation of the shortcoming, you need to assure those wronged that you will do everything possible to make sure that it will not happen again.

4. **Restoration**: Finally, a genuine act of contrition requires you to make a pledge to help the person you wronged to recover and, if appropriate, to provide compensation to her for harm you cannot remedy. In other words, your apology must communicate the desire to make a person whole again (certainly without creating the impression that you are throwing money at a problem to make it go away).

This formula for contrition has applications for you in Corporate America, in small business America and in everyday life. There is tremendous value in making apologies and seeking redemption, provided it is sincere and is accompanied by corrective action. In so doing, you acknowledge your wrongdoing and help others to forgive.

Most importantly, by having contrition you bolster the trust others have in you that you will not harm them again.

Foundational Networking Extra
Charlie Hustle

Consider the man called Charlie Hustle, Pete Rose. Rose was a Major League Baseball player from 1963 to 1986, most notably with the Cincinnati Reds. In that time span, he won three World Series rings, three batting titles, one Most Valuable Player Award, two Gold Gloves, a Rookie of the Year Award and made 17 appearances in the All-Star game at an unmatched five different positions (First Base, Second Base, Third Base, Left Field and Right Field). In addition, he is the all-time Major League leader in games played (3,562), at bats (14,053) and hits (4,256).

In August 1989, only three years after he retired as an active player, Rose agreed to a lifetime ban from baseball amidst accusations that he gambled on baseball games while playing for and managing the Reds. After years of public denial, in 2004 he admitted to betting on, but not against, the Reds. As part of his admission, Rose stated he was sorry for betting on baseball.

While the words were there, the intent of Rose's apology rang hollow. There are only a few who believed that his apology was an expression of true regret and remorse. In fact, most believe that he was primarily motivated to apologize by a desire to have the Baseball Writers Association admit him into the Baseball Hall of Fame – whose rules prohibited induction for those banned from baseball.

Most baseball experts agree that the Baseball Writers Association will never induct Pete Rose into the Baseball Hall of Fame. Most experts also agree that this denial is not because he bet on baseball or subsequently lied about that fact. The reason the Baseball Writers Association will not induct Pete Rose into the Baseball Hall of Fame is because Rose has never had true contrition with respect to his actions.

Personal Responsbility

"He must be pure who would blame another."
— Danish Proverb

Life is not an endless succession of forward progress. You have days when good things happen and days when great things happen. And days when things go terribly wrong.

It may be that a valued client chooses not to do business with you anymore. It may be that someone gives you directions to the wrong golf course. It may be that your four-year-old son or daughter spills grape juice on the new white carpet. In these moments, it is all too easy for you to lash out and point the finger at someone else:

"Obviously, engineering has not kept us on the cutting edge."

"I specifically told them that I needed directions to Oak Haven, not Oakhurst."

"What are you doing with your juice in the living room?"

This is a seemingly natural reaction. The problem is that no one likes to be on the receiving end of blame. Certainly, this is understandable if the person has done nothing worthy of blame. However, even if the person has made a mistake, the guilt over their actions or inactions is penance enough. Thus, your blame, no matter how you might candy coat it, serves only to add insult to injury.

Reflect back on the last time that someone lashed out and blamed you for something that went awry. Whether you were culpable or not, your immediate reaction was a defensive one. You may have lashed back or pointed the finger elsewhere. In any event, even if it was only temporary, at that moment you did not like the person blaming you. More importantly, however, the trust you had in that person was impaired.

Knowing this, you need to be cautious in how and when you blame others for those occasional misfortunes you encounter. This is not to suggest that you avoid correcting others' oversights, slip-ups or blunders. You should. This is part of helping others grow and is imperative to anyone in a leadership position, the first and foremost of which is parenthood. However, there is a stark difference between accusing someone of an error and guiding him toward improvement.

Nevertheless, you need to develop the attitude that whenever something goes awry you have some culpability. Then, long before you consider doling out blame, you should develop the habit of first carefully examining your contribution to the situation. The fact of the matter is that under any circumstances, there is probably a little blame in there for you – even where the culpable person is obvious.

Consider if your son or daughter spills his or her grape juice on the white carpet. While you were not the one who spilled the grape juice, you can find fault for your own actions or inactions. For example, you could have given them a different cup – one with a cover or a larger base. You could have not filled the cup so full. You could have done a better job watching over your child's movements as well as where the cup was placed. While these realizations may not eliminate your frustration as you clean up, knowing your own shortcomings certainly tempers it.

This same logic is effective in your professional life as well. When a member of the sales staff falls short of her quota, certainly she is somewhat responsible for the failure. You can share in the letdown, however. Perhaps your motivation was lacking. Perhaps your training and guidance was less effective than you thought. Perhaps the quota you set was unrealistic given the circumstances. Perhaps ... perhaps ... perhaps. In all likelihood, you can share the blame a dozen other ways for this situation alone.

While people need to know and understand their part in failures, they need to feel supported in efforts to correct those failures. You can do this by sharing with others your own culpability in a failure as part of correcting them. For example, "It is unfortunate that you did not hit your sales quota this month. In thinking through it, there are some things I could be doing better as your sales manager, such as … Having said that, I think you know that you have some things you can be improving on as well, such as …"

Yes, every mistake provides an opportunity for learning. Thus, if you have openly blamed others – whether or not they deserved it – understand that these people (as well as those who witness it) become less comfortable and trusting of you.

While they may trust your abilities as a professional, they will become unsure of the repercussions of being associated with you when things are not going well. This mistrust will then serve to deteriorate your integrity in their eyes. In the end, it will have an adverse impact on your foundational networking.

Foundational Networking Extra
Measure Twice

Over the last several years, I have taken an interest in home improvement projects. Although I am relatively proficient at home improvement, it was not always this way. In the beginning, I made my share of mistakes (and occasionally still do).

With every mistake, however, I learn something. While every mistake holds a lesson, not all lessons relate entirely back to home improvement. For example, one of the first projects I undertook at our new house was finishing the basement – converting it from a rough storage area to living space.

Finishing a basement requires, among lots of other things, that I frame the walls with two-by-four boards by installing a series of boards horizontally along the perimeter of the floor and ceiling and then installing boards vertically around the room.

Early on a Saturday morning, I started the process of framing the basement along with a trusty assistant, my then-five-year-old son, Lucas. While I did not expect my son to be of much assistance, he wanted to help. Besides, I learned much of what I know about home improvement by watching and helping my father. In addition, after being at work all week, I thought a little father-son bonding time would be nice.

Nevertheless, my son's presence complicated the project. I had to keep him involved, but at the same time keep him out of harm's way. My plan to do this was simple. I would cut the boards and put them in place. Then I would only partially hammer in the nails – just enough to secure the boards. My son could then occupy himself by hammering in the nails the remainder of the way.

When framing, some areas go rather quickly. However, in other areas, the process is more complicated. These areas take more time and more thought. Toward the end of the day, I embarked on one of these areas. Although I was feeling good about all that I had accomplished, I was down to my final few boards. As a result, I was feeling pressure to do a good job and not make a mistake.

At this point, I was working to frame around an area where there was a window. I measured the window opening and then I set about making my cuts. When I completed the cuts, I carried the pieces over to the window and prepared to secure them to the boards I already had in place. Almost immediately, I realized that I had made a mistake. I had cut the boards too short. The lumber was wasted, and as I had no more, I could not finish the job that day.

All this while, my son worked away hammering at the last bit of nail that I left for him to drive into the wood. Like a little jackhammer, he struck at each nail a hundred times or so – sometimes making contact and sometimes not. In any event, he was making quite a racket.

In complete frustration – the noise, the mistake and my inability to complete the job – I lashed out at my son, "LUCAS! Stop hammering. You made me make a mistake." My son stopped right away and looked at me in bewilderment. He did not know what he did wrong, and soon tears started to well up in his eyes.

At that moment, my anger and frustration melted away and I said, "Sorry." After all, he did nothing wrong, other than miss the nail 50 percent of the times he swung at it. And whatever he was doing did not add to the issue I created. The mistake was entirely mine.

This situation yielded two lessons. The first was a standard carpenter's mantra: "Measure twice; cut once." The second had value beyond my foray into home improvement: We need to be cautious in blaming others for anything. In fact, the lesson is similar – before you set about blaming someone else, think twice, blame once.

Forgiveness

"The weak can never forgive.
Forgiveness is the attribute of the strong."
– Mahatma Gandhi

Forgiveness is the mental or spiritual process of ceasing to feel resentment or anger toward another for a perceived offense, and at the same time ceasing to demand punishment or restitution. Whether absolving for a near genocide or a minor affront, forgiveness is a powerful thing. The simple act of forgiving provides tremendous benefits.

First, it takes incredible energy to hold on to the pent-up resentment and anger of a grudge. In essence, resentment toward others allows them to live rent-free in our heads by consuming valuable thought and creativity while at the same time offering no value in return. Forgiving others allows us to divert this energy to more productive and creative endeavors.

Additionally, studies show that people who forgive are happier and healthier than those who hold resentments. Researchers theorize that this is because the bitterness of a grudge is like a mental poison. This mental poison does not hurt anyone but the person harboring the resentment. This resentment depletes strength and prevents wounds from healing.

From the perspective of foundational networking, holding on to grudges and resentment serves to undermine your integrity. You need to think about that if another has wronged you and you are having trouble forgiving the offense.

Consider the person who declares, "I will never forgive them for what they did!" Often, the offense associated with this defiance to forgiving is nothing egregious. It might be an unwarranted rude comment. Or it might be a betrayal, whether personal or professional. In any event, these infractions are nothing compared to many of the atrocities that people have endured and forgiven others for.

How do you react whenever someone resists forgiving another? You likely tense up. You instantly become uneasy interacting with that person. While you might not be the target of their disdain, you cannot help but question to yourself, "What do I need to do to avoid being subject to this eternal contempt?"

With that in the back of your mind, you devote incredible energy to choosing your words carefully and become slow to act for fear of conflicting with this person. In a sense, you do not trust this person or at least do not trust yourself being around him. You become uncomfortable and stressed. Over time, you seek to diminish this discomfort, which is done by minimizing your interaction with this person.

Knowing this, you must not be the person who is unable to forgive. Develop the attitudes and habits that allow you to let go of those times when others wronged you. Forgive their transgressions. Whatever they did, the damage is done. You cannot change that by holding on to anger and resentment.

This is not to say that you need to forget. For example, if someone in business fails to pay you, the concept of forgiveness does not suggest that you must continue to do business with him. As a competent businessperson, you need to make judgments based on past occurrences – both good and bad.

It is not inappropriate to remember the episodes when someone wronged you. This is simply human nature. While remembering is acceptable, you need to work to ensure that the associated anger and resentment leave your mind as soon as reasonably possible.

Foundational Networking Extra

Left To Forgive

In the Spring of 1994, Immaculée Ilibagiza was home on leave as a student from the Rwanda National University. On April 5th, she was having dinner with her family like they often did. At that dinner, her older brother, Damascene, implored Immaculée's father to move the family away. At the time, signs of trouble had been mounting with the Hutu – one of three native peoples of Rwanda who at the time held majority control of the country.

Her brother was simply attempting to protect the family – who were Tutsi, another of the native people – from what he surmised would be eventual violence. He feared that the Tutsi would be targeted by the rival Hutu. Damascene was right.

On April 6, 1994, a plane carrying Rwanda's Hutu president, Juvenal Habyarimana, was struck by missiles, killing all on board. Almost immediately a well-organized campaign by Hutu extremists against Tutsis followed. Hutu government ministers began openly threatening Tutsis on state radio: "We will kill them [Tutsis], their brothers and sisters. We will kill, and they will never find anyone."

In the early days, hundreds of people crowded around the home of Immaculée's father. He was the chief administrator of a Roman Catholic school and a figure of authority in the region. Her father, who had lived through two previous civil wars, expressed confidence that order would be restored. For that reason, when the family had a clear chance to flee Rwanda on the day of the assassination, they did not take it.

Shortly thereafter, the situation became dire. Within days, access to Lake Kivu, an escape route to the Congo, was closed. Hutu officials began summoning Tutsis out of their homes to gather in stadiums and churches, where they were eventually massacred. Immaculée and her family were resolved to the situation. They would not be fleeing Rwanda. Rather, they would have to face the situation as it unfolded.

Immaculée's father directed the members of the family to disperse. He arranged for Immaculée to hide in the home of a local Lutheran pastor, an ethnic Hutu named Simeon Nzabahimana. Early on the morning of April 11th, she was taken to Simeon's home and told to hide in a 3-foot by 4-foot bathroom with seven other women. This was assumed to be only a temporary situation, lasting only a day or two. However, the eight women would spend the next three months hiding in this one room.

On July 7th, 1994, after most of the killing had ended, Immaculée and the other women emerged from their bathroom hiding place. It was only at this time that she was able to piece together what had truly occurred to her native people and family members. In just 100 days, an estimated 800,000 to 1,000,000 Tutsis were killed. An estimated 60,000 Tutsis – 80 percent of the native population – were dead in the Kibuye region, a remote western province where the killing was particularly efficient.

Of her immediate family, her father was shot by soldiers shortly after Immaculée went into hiding. Her mother was killed by machete. And her younger brother was among hundreds of Tutsis who had gathered in a local stadium in search of food and were executed. Her older brother, who tried in vain to have the family flee Rwanda, was able to provide Immaculée with a written account of the first month of the genocide. However, he was killed while attempting to flee via Lake Kivu. In addition, Immaculée also lost four grandparents and seven uncles.

More or less, she lost an entire family along with hundreds of thousands of other Tutsis. This would leave most of us bitter and vengeful toward those responsible, and even via those who were negligent in not taking action to prevent the genocide. After this, however, she became a member of the United Nations Development Program and currently is a full time author and speaker, devoting her life to sharing the importance of the virtues of understanding and forgiveness. In fact, Immaculée shares her miraculous story of how she survived during the 1994 Rwanda genocide in her book *Left to Tell: Discovering God Amidst the Rwandan Holocaust*.

In *Left to Tell*, Immaculée discloses an epiphany she had toward those Hutu who were slaughtering her fellow Tutsis.

It was no use—my prayers felt hollow. A war had started in my soul, and I could no longer pray to a God of love with a heart full of hatred. I tried again, praying for Him to forgive the killers, but deep down I couldn't believe that they deserved it at all. It tormented me...I tried to pray for them myself, but I felt like I was praying for the devil. *Please open my heart, Lord, and show me how to forgive. I'm not strong enough to squash my hatred—they've wronged us all so much...my hatred is so heavy that it could crush me. Touch my heart, Lord, and show me how to forgive.*

I struggled with the dilemma for hours on end. I prayed late into the night, all through the next day, and the day after that, and the day after that. I prayed all week, scarcely taking food or water. I couldn't remember when or how long I'd slept, and was only vaguely aware of time passing.

One night I heard screaming not far from the house, and then a baby crying. The killers must have slain the mother and left her infant to die in the road. The child wailed all night; by morning, its cries were feeble and sporadic, and by nightfall, it was silent. I heard dogs snarling nearby and shivered to think how that baby's life had ended. I prayed for God to receive the child's innocent soul, and then asked Him, *How can I forgive people who would do such a thing to an infant?*

I heard His answer as clearly as if we'd been sitting in the same room chatting: *You are all my children...and the baby is with Me now.*

It was such a simple sentence, but it was the answer to the prayers I'd been lost in for days.

The killers were like children. Yes, they were barbaric creatures who would have to be punished severely for their actions, but they were still children. They were cruel, vicious, and dangerous, as kids sometimes can be, but nevertheless, they were children. They saw, but didn't understand the terrible harm they'd inflicted. They'd blindly hurt others without thinking, they'd hurt their Tutsi brothers and sisters, they'd hurt God—and they didn't understand how badly they were hurting themselves. Their minds had been infected with the evil that had spread across the country, but their souls weren't evil. Despite their atrocities, they were children of God, and I could forgive a child, although it would not be easy...especially when that child was trying to kill me.

In God's eyes, the killers were part of His family, deserving of love and forgiveness. I knew that I couldn't ask God to love me if I was unwilling to love His children. At that moment, I prayed for the killers, for their sins to be forgiven. I prayed that God would lead them to recognize the horrific error of their ways before their life on Earth ended—before they were called to account for their mortal sins.

I held on to my father's rosary and asked God to help me, and again I heard His voice: *Forgive them; they know not what they do.*

I took a crucial step toward forgiving the killers that day. My anger was draining from me—I'd opened my heart to God, and He'd touched it with His infinite love. For the first time, I pitied the killers. I asked God to forgive their sins and turn their souls toward His beautiful Light.

That night I prayed with a clear conscience and a clean heart. For the first time since I entered the bathroom, I slept in peace.

The story of Immaculée Ilibagiza is amazing. Here was a young woman living a seemingly normal life – enjoying time with her family while home from college for a visit in early spring. Overnight her world was cast into turmoil. Then before the summer was over her family and upwards of a million fellow Tutsis were slaughtered. Clearly, she was irreparably harmed and irreversibly bereaved. Despite this, she found the compassion and courage to forgive those who inflicted this suffering.

If under the circumstances of the Rwandan genocide Immaculée Ilibagiza can find the capacity to forgive, then as she states in her book, "Anyone in the world can learn to forgive those who have injured them, however great or small that injury may be." Immaculée should make us realize that we cannot forgive others often enough or quickly enough.

Open Mindedness

"Don't judge a man by his opinions, but what his opinions have made of him."
— Georg Christoph Lichtenberg

Whatever your opinions, remember they are not definitive facts. Your opinions are only your perspective, based on your perception of how you see the world.

With that, endeavor to share your opinions responsibly. There is nothing wrong with being passionate, outspoken and remarkably confident with respect to your opinion. You can also carefully lay out your arguments, complete with whatever sustaining facts that serve to support your position.

However, remember that the role of giving your opinion is sharing your perception and perspective. At the same time, be completely unconcerned as to whether or not you sway anyone else to your view.

Consider two different types of people, each with their own attitudes and habits related to sharing opinions. With whom would you prefer to associate?

There is the person who politely listens to your opinion attentively, doing her best to understand your position. Then, when the time is appropriate she might respectfully share her opinion.

Even though the two of you do not agree, this person can quietly accept that an opposite opinion could exist. From here, the person has the maturity to carry the relationship forward by finding commonality on another topic. Or if that is not possible, she is able to arrange a friendly parting, agreeing to disagree on the conflict in question.

Then there is the person who wastes little time in sharing her opinion. While she is mildly interested in your opinion, she is primarily interested in whether or not you agree.

If you do not, she instantly switches tactics, trying to change your opinion. The person will keep after you with re-packaged argument after re- packaged argument or statistic after statistic.

The person is dead set on getting you to see it her way. "No, you cannot possibly think that ... and this is why ..." She will carry on and on as if to say "if you do not agree with my opinion, you cannot possibly be fully informed." This person simply cannot rest until she has exhausted every possible means of swaying your opinion to hers.

Certainly, the first person is someone with whom you would be more comfortable associating. You could trust that your interactions with her will be open and honest. Additionally, you can expect conversations to be somewhat enlightening as you are less guarded and more interested in this person's view. In any respect, by no means will your relations be confrontational. On one point, you may disagree, but it is only one point.

Regarding the second person, what are you supposed to do? Certainly, you cannot hope to change her. For the most part, these people are fully mature men and women. This opinionated nature may be genetic or acquired somewhere along the way. In either case, they are who they are, for better or for worse.

The most important thing that you can do is to commit to not becoming one of them. If you attempt to force your opinions on other people or even aggressively advocate them, in a way, you violate the trust of others by making them less comfortable around you.

When you act in this manner, even those around you whose opinions are in line with yours will be less trusting of and more uncomfortable with you. This is because they will be wary of the day when their perspective might be at odds with yours.

In addition, if you carry on in this manner, they will become uneasy about introducing you to others. This is because they will be afraid that your interaction with other parts of their network might escalate into a heated confrontation about seemingly minor differences. While they can always walk away or somehow serve to mitigate the situation, they would be fearful that your actions with others might somehow be associated with them.

This is not to say that you need to concede your position on issues or ideas in hopes of placating your network. You do not have to agree with anyone. You do, however, need to accept that others have a different point of view.

Accepting is merely understanding that others have a different perspective and respecting that they have a right to it. This is agreeing to disagree.

Is agreeing to disagree reasonable in the real world of today? Absolutely. It is completely in line with the Golden Rule: "Do unto others as you would have them do unto you." After all, you do not want someone to cajole you into changing your opinion. Thus, it is reasonable to assume that no one else does either.

Is this notion of agreeing to disagree realistic? Again, the answer is absolutely. It has to be. Life would become very lonely if the only people you had in your network were those who agreed with you on every front. Effective foundational networking requires you to be tolerant of differing perspectives. After all, we cannot all affiliate with the same political party or affiliate with a political party at all. We cannot all believe in the same religion or even believe in one at all. We cannot all think that the same brand of pizza (or any other product) is the best.

If we all thought the same and believed the same, there would be no choice in the world and no competition in the economy. Without choice and competition, there would be no freedom and no innovation.

The fact on opinions is that our diversity in perspective gives our networks value and strength. We should embrace our differing views and not rail against them.

Foundational Networking Extra
Six Blind Men & An Elephant

A long time ago in the valley of the Brahmaputra River in India there lived six men who were much inclined to boast of their wit and lore. Though they were no longer young and had all been blind since birth, they would compete with each other to see who could tell the tallest tale.

One day, however, they fell to arguing. The object of their dispute was the elephant. Now, since each was blind, none had ever seen that mighty beast of which so many tales are told. So, to satisfy their minds and settle the dispute, they decided to go and seek out an elephant.

Having hired a young guide, Dookiram by name, they set out early one morning in single file along the forest track, each placing hands on the back of the man in front. It was not long before they came to a forest clearing where a huge bull elephant, quite tame, was standing contemplating his menu for the day.

The six blind men became quite excited; at last they would satisfy their minds. Thus it was that the men took turns to investigate the elephant's shape and form. As all six men were blind, none of them could see the whole elephant and approached the elephant from different directions. After encountering the elephant, each man proclaimed in turn:

- 'O my brothers,' the first man at once cried out, 'it is as sure as I am wise that this elephant is like a great mud wall baked hard in the sun.'

- 'Now, my brothers,' the second man exclaimed with a cry of dawning recognition, 'I can tell you what shape this elephant is – he is exactly like a spear.' The others smiled in disbelief.

- 'Why, dear brothers, do you not see,' said the third man – 'this elephant is very much like a rope,' he shouted.

- 'Ha, I thought as much,' the fourth man declared excitedly, 'This elephant much resembles a serpent.' The others snorted their contempt.

- 'Good gracious, brothers,' the fifth man called out, 'even a blind man can see what shape the elephant resembles most. Why he's mightily like a fan.'

- At last, it was the turn of the sixth old fellow and he proclaimed, 'This sturdy pillar, brothers mine, feels exactly like the trunk of a great areca palm tree.' Of course, no one believed him.

Their curiosity satisfied, they all followed the guide, Dookiram, back to the village. Once there, seated beneath a waving palm, the six blind men began disputing loud and long. Each now had his own opinion, firmly based on his own experience, of what an elephant is really like. For after all, each had felt the elephant for himself and knew that he was right.

While none of the blind men was completely right and none of the blind men was completely wrong, each approached the situation from a different perspective.

Tactfulness

> "Tact is the ability to describe others
> as they see themselves."
> — *Abraham Lincoln*

A reality of life is that there are unpleasant things. There is the subordinate at work who seems to be perpetually unhappy. There is the vendor who got the order all wrong, again. There is the neighbor who has overly rowdy kids and a dog that barks excessively.

Another reality of life is that often you need to address these unpleasant situations. You need to talk with the subordinate about his lack of contentment. You need to address the vendor about the botched orders. For your sanity, you need to speak with the neighbor about the noise coming from her house.

In facing up to these realities, remember that it is not what you do that matters. From a perspective of effective foundational networking, what matters is how you do it.

How you do things is merely tact and it is nothing more than a form of interpersonal diplomacy. It is when you intend to induce change or communicate potentially hurtful information without offending the person. Using tact requires that you exhibit consideration, kindness and reason.

In successfully using tact to deal with others, adopt the attitude that it is important for you to rise above difficult situations and exhibit professionalism or a heightened level of maturity. Remember that in addressing difficult situations, it is not your role to make the other party feel bad or get them to concede guilt with respect to shortcomings. It is simply about rectifying the situation.

In addressing the error-prone vendor, you can bark out, "Why do you keep screwing up our orders?" In so doing, you only serve to inflame the situation. It makes you the aggressor and immediately puts the vendor on the defensive. Your reactive statement accomplishes nothing productive. Successfully using tact requires that you develop the habit of reflecting on situations before you say or do anything. It does not matter that the person is completely absent-minded or wholly incapable of servicing you. It is not your role to try to establish any of this. It is your role to correct the situation.

An alternative approach to addressing the vendor might be, "We seem to be having more than our share of trouble getting our orders filled accurately. Is there something on our end that could help resolve this?" You are not confronting the person. Instead, you focus on the situation.

Reflect for a moment on a situation where you were the brunt of a tactless person's comments or actions – "Quite frankly, your management skills or experience are inferior and therefore we could not promote you." How did it make you feel? Whatever the situation, chances are his comments did not endear him to you. You probably immediately liked him less and distrusted him more.

Consider another situation (or even imagine the same situation), where you were handled in a more diplomatic fashion – "Unfortunately, we were not able to promote you at this time. We felt that it would be best if we allow you some additional time to develop your management skills and gain some more experience." How did that make you feel? While no one enjoys receiving disappointing news, you can likely accept this without feeling defeated. In turn, your feelings toward the person telling you are much more positive.

The lesson is that the use of tact – where we focus on situations and not individuals – will serve to advance you from a foundational networking perspective.

Foundational Networking Exercise

Consider an unpleasant situation you need to address. What are two or three tactful ways to rectify the situation?

Unpleasant Situation: _____

_____

_____

1. _____

_____

2. _____

_____

3. _____

_____

Appropriate Motivation

> "The glue that holds all relationships together –
> including the relationship between
> the leader and the led – is trust,
> and trust is based on integrity."
> *– Brian Tracy*

Much of your success in life depends upon your ability to motivate others. You motivated others to play with you as a child, whether that entailed sharing time on an activity or trading NFL player cards. You motivated others to date you as a teenager and marry you as a young adult. You motivated others to hire you or do business with you. Motivation is essential to a healthy social and professional life.

However, when you motivate others, you need to remember that motivation is nothing more than finding objectives that are good for both others and yourself and then encouraging others to undertake the actions that will help achieve those objectives.

Motivation has a dark side, though. This is simply the temptation to motivate others toward goals and objectives that serve your interests, but are knowingly not in their best interest. This is known as manipulation.

If you are honest with yourself, you will admit that there has been a time when you were tempted to manipulate someone else. As you are only human, these temptations are natural – you want to advance yourself, personally or professionally (and that does not always take others into consideration). However, you need to develop the attitudes and habits that ensure that you resist these temptations.

After all, chances are there was a time or two when others manipulated you (or at least tried). Perhaps they tried to sell you something you did not need. Perhaps, it was less obvious – where they attempted to get you to do something, such as attend a seminar, where they knew it would not benefit you, but your presence would benefit them.

Whether the manipulation was overt or subtle, how did their actions make you feel? You probably felt a little cheated if they succeeded in the manipulation. Moreover, whether or not they were successful, you probably felt used.

How did you feel toward the people who perpetrated the manipulations? Instantly, you felt a sense of disillusionment. You might even have questioned, "Do I really know these people?" Moreover, you began to feel a disdain for the people, even if it was only temporarily. This disenchantment and disdain manifested itself in a loss of trust.

There are those who will couch manipulative behavior as "good salesmanship" or simply taking care of oneself. But manipulation is dishonest and it is arguably lying. In any event, it is wrong and it will deteriorate and ultimately destroy even the best of relationships.

Much of your success in life does depend upon your ability to motivate others. For this to work, when you motivate others you need to be ever vigilant that you consider the best interests of others as well. If you do not, you not only hurt your ability to motivate others in the future, but you also impair your foundational networking.

Foundational Networking Exercise

Identify three situations where someone attempted (or succeeded in) manipulating you. What is your current relationship with the person? How well regarded is he in his field or profession?

1. _____

2. _____

3. _____

Conscientious Influence

"All human actions have one or more of these seven causes: chance, nature, compulsion, habit, reason, passion, and desire."
— Aristotle

Along the same lines as appropriately motivating the actions of others, foundational networking requires that you use your position to influence others in a responsible manner.

There are those who will use their position of authority or power in an irresponsible manner. Consider the situation in which an employer might intimate to his staff that opportunities might not be forthcoming to those who do not support the chosen charity. Then, consider the situation in which a client coerces vendors to take a particular unwanted action with an implied or overt threat of loss of business.

You misuse your authority any time you use your power or position to coerce the undesired action or inaction of someone who feels under the influence of your power or position. That could be a subordinate or a peer. In certain situations, it could even be a superior.

Certainly, you might argue that there is nothing wrong with this. You might argue that employers continually use threats to motivate the actions of their staff. You might further argue that the vendor is free at any point to find a new client should he or she not like the pressure that a client is exerting. You might assert that this sort of behavior happens in many different situations, each of which is acceptable. After all, this is a free market society and it is just business and that is the way it has always been.

That is true. It is just business. There is nothing illegal about an employer pressuring employees to support a favorite charity. Moreover, clients make demands – sometimes ridiculous demands – of vendors. It is just business.

While it is business, it is bad business. Place yourself in the shoes of the employee, the vendor or anyone else under pressure to do something. In the short run, you may feel compelled to remain in the situation – supporting a charity with which you have little interest or capitulating to onerous demands.

In the end, there is no real relationship beyond what the immediate situation compels. You neither like nor trust the employer, the client or the person behind the pressure. When that situation passes (or worse, the tables turn), none of these people can count on you as being a productive and functioning part of their network. They have irresponsibly used their position and, in so doing, violated your trust.

In this regard, there is no truth to the statement "that is the way it has always been." There are those individuals who make a practice of misusing the authority that their position gives them. However, this cannot be an indictment of everyone.

There are people who have power and position and make nothing but an upstanding use of those attributes. They do not threaten the employment of subordinates who do not hold their views or those who might not support their cause. They do not attempt to coerce the action (or inaction) of any supplier or vendor – they only expect good service in the normal course of business.

In addition, even if "that is the way it has always been," that does not make it right. For centuries, early Americans used the labor of slaves to drive the economy. No one would argue today that this practice was right. However, up until the *Emancipation Proclamation*, "that was the way it had always been."

Moreover, "that is the way it has always been" certainly does not mean "that is the way it always has to be." Just because an employer, manager or client (or anyone else) may have exerted some form of coercion on you does not mean you need to continue the practice. You can commit to being one of those people who has power and position, but is widely known for making nothing but an upstanding use of those attributes.

Sound foundational networking requires that you become the person with whom you want to associate. At the same time, it requires that you avoid becoming the person you would despise.

People will go to great lengths to follow and support you, provided you use your position responsibly. People will also go to great lengths to undermine you if you do not.

Foundational Networking Exercise

Identify three situations where someone whose authority or influence you were under misused his or her position with respect to you. What is your current relationship to the person? How well regarded is the individual in his field or profession?

1. _____

2. _____

3. _____

Foundational Networking Improvement

> "Our lives improve only when we take chances
> – and the first and most difficult risk we take
> is to be honest with ourselves."
> — *Walter Anderson*

At this time, you might be saying to yourself: "Okay, okay. I get it. The basis for a productive network is simply being a good person – be generous, positive and honorable. I get it. That is foundational networking. So what? I am already all of those things. I am a good person."

Before you rest on the image you have for yourself, consider what Harry Beckwith indicated in his book *Selling the Invisible* – we, as humans, think we are better than we are. In fact, Beckwith cites some statistics to support his conclusion:

- 60 percent of students rate themselves in the top 10 percent of the class; or,

- 94 percent of university professors say they are doing a better job than their average colleague; or,

- Most people consider themselves good looking.

Psychologists refer to this as the "Lake Wobegon Effect" after Garrison Keillor's famous show sign-off from his fictional hometown, Lake Wobegon: "Where the women are strong, the men are good looking, and all the children are above average."

So, you have concluded that you have the qualities of presence, altruism and integrity. Now think for a moment. In your mind, can you point to someone who does not have presence or someone who lacks integrity? Can you point a mental finger at someone who you would not consider altruistic? Chances are you can conjure up an image of someone who lacks one or more of the elements essential to foundational networking.

Therefore, while you consider yourself highly effective at foundational networking, you know someone who is not for one or more reasons.

Here is where it gets enlightening. How likely is it that someone you have a mental finger pointed at is one of the same people who has concluded for herself that she has qualities of presence, altruism and integrity? Would you agree that the odds are more than likely? You probably know someone who has a substantially inflated opinion of her personal skills.

Now, what are the chances that someone has a finger pointed at you? What are the chances that someone considers your foundational networking skills not quite as proficient as you think they are? Considering the Lake Wobegon Effect, the odds are relatively good.

Assume for a moment that someone has dubbed you as lacking presence, not being altruistic or short on integrity (or worse yet, all three). What would be your reaction? It would probably be something like, "They really do not know me. They have misjudged me or they simply are not privy to the times when I have demonstrated presence, altruism and integrity." Following this declaration, you would likely cite specific examples.

On the other hand, maybe they know you better than you think. Maybe, while you can cite examples of when you have exhibited characteristics of sound foundational networking, your overall reputation is lacking in one or more of these traits.

How could this be? How could you have misjudged yourself so significantly? The answer is that it is only human nature. If you have any sort of self-esteem at all, you tend to look at yourself in a more favorable light than might actually be the case.

The reality is that no one is perfect. There are extremely generous people in the world. Not one of them gives to every cause or in every situation. Alternatively, there are extremely selfish people. However, they have all given of themselves in one situation or another.

Regarding presence, no one can possibly always display positive personality attributes. On the flip side, even the most downtrodden and demoralized person has a moment when optimistic spirits shine through an otherwise gloomy disposition.

Finally, everyone has a degree of integrity. The reality is that for many it is of a more heightened degree than others have. There are good people who do bad things and there are bad people who do good things.

The point is that none of the components of foundational networking is an all or nothing thing. That is, there are not simply those who cast a presence and those who do not (or those who are altruistic and those who are not … or those with integrity and those without). For each, it is a matter of degree.

Therefore, you do cast a presence, you are altruistic and you have integrity. The question is, to what degree? Moreover, how can you further develop each quality?

How do you develop something that you do not know needs to be developed? If you are only human and for that reason under the spell of the Lake Wobegon Effect, how do you set about improving your foundational networking – something that you did not perceive as needing to be improved.

To address this further, you need to revisit the book *Selling The Invisible*. The author, Harry Beckwith, addresses ideas and insights for marketing services such as technology, legal, accounting, financial and logistics. Certainly, business and personal relationships with others, for many of us, are the only services we have to offer. Therefore, in part, *Selling The Invisible* has clear applications to foundational networking.

Beckwith, a renowned consultant on advertising and marketing to some of America's best service companies, says that the first step to marketing any service is to fix it. In other words, it makes little sense to draft press releases, formulate ad copy or secure a prospect list unless you deliver service spectacularly.

A business will find that fixing a service is easier said than done, however. This is not to say that fixing a problem is difficult. The difficult part is in recognizing the problems a business needs to fix. Businesses are no different from humans, mainly because humans run them. They are subject to the Lake Wobegon Effect. In short, business owners tend to think their service is better than the consensus opinion.

Beckwith's solution for fixing a service – one which a business would likely consider not broken under normal circumstances – is to assume that the service is sub-par or flawed. He encourages businesses to focus on every aspect of their service to determine where problems exist and fix them. And maybe the service is not as awful as a business owner might assume. That is irrelevant. The fact is that the service is not perfect. By focusing on it, the business cannot help but improve the service in the process.

Therefore, to begin the process of improving your foundational networking, you need to take a critical look at the underlying elements of your presence, altruism and integrity and assume they are flawed.

In the case of presence, make a serious examination of this element, viewing it as if you were looking at someone else – someone you might not be fond of. Then do the same for your level of altruism and integrity. If you honestly approach each element of foundational networking in the manner proposed by Beckwith, you will not be able to avoid improving your foundational networking.

The point is that no matter who you are, you cast a presence, are altruistic and you have a degree of integrity. As such, you have and will continue to embark on foundational networking.

No matter what you have done (or failed to do), it is not as effective as it could be. Thus, there is always merit in attempting to improve your foundational networking.

After all, you are not perfect. You never have been. From a foundational networking perspective, at times, your spirits are down and optimism is off. On occasion, you simply are not as generous or thoughtful as you could be. In certain moments, your integrity is lacking.

The imperfections of your foundational networking have been with you for a long time. The shortcomings in your presence, altruism and integrity did not occur last week, last month or last year. These flaws did not occur upon your entrance into the professional world. These deficiencies have been with you in one degree or another for your entire life.

You cannot go back and compensate for that time when your enthusiasm left something to be desired. You cannot undo the times when you missed an opportunity to be more altruistic. You are not able to reverse your lapses in judgment that caused others to perceive you as lacking integrity.

Take consolation in the fact that you are not alone. Everyone's networking skills are limited by the imperfection of their foundational networking and everyone has been plagued for years to one degree or another by these imperfections.

The difference, however, is that you are now privy to the impact of the Lake Wobegon Effect. You know you may not be as proficient at foundational networking as you might have thought. You know there is room for improvement.

This is the first step toward improving your foundational networking – acknowledging that there is room for improvement. Understanding alone, however, is meaningless unless you move beyond it and commit to actual improvement.

The most important step in improvement is the first one – getting started. Getting started on improving anything involves looking for ways to measure the improvement, which will allow you to take advantage of the Hawthorne Effect.

What is the Hawthorne Effect? From 1927 to 1932, Professor Elton Mayo examined the relationship between productivity and working conditions at the Western Electric Hawthorne Works in Cicero, Illinois, near Chicago. Mayo started these experiments by examining how lighting affected productivity.

When Mayo increased the brightness of the lights, productivity increased. When he increased it again, productivity further increased. This pattern continued for several more trials. Mayo and the executives of Western Electric were excited as they felt they were on to something.

Then Mayo broke from the trend he was following and he dimmed the lights on the Western Electric employees. To his astonishment, productivity increased again. He immediately revised his hypothesis. The brightness of the lights did not affect productivity of workers. What affected productivity was the mere fact that someone was monitoring and measuring it.

How does this relate to your foundational networking? Again, the answer is "that which you measure you will improve." If you monitor and measure the various aspects of foundational networking – presence, altruism and integrity – that focus alone with ensure that you improve these elements.

This can be problematic, however. How do you quantify presence? How do you monitor altruism? How do you compute integrity? None of these is easy to measure as none is quantifiable. Nevertheless, you can gauge these principles.

Understand that there is a formula for becoming successful at anything. Conversely stated, success in any meaningful endeavor is not a function of chance or dumb luck. Success is simply a function of appropriately completing certain elements or objectives. In short, if you complete the designated objectives, you are likely to be successful at a particular endeavor.

For example, consider health. If it is your goal to become healthy and maintain your health, there are certain objectives you must undertake. First, you need to eat a reasonably balanced diet with plenty of fruits and vegetables. Second, you need to get a reasonable amount of exercise throughout each week. Finally, you should drink eight glasses of water each day. If you do these things, in all likelihood, you will be healthy.

Your health will not occur simply by accident. Nor will your success at anything of substance be because of chance or dumb luck. This includes improving your foundational networking. You need to seek to complete the objectives that will ensure your success.

Merely declaring that you will set forth to complete the necessary objectives to achieve success is not enough, however. For example, individuals who declare a New Year's resolution are successful only four percent of the time. According to research, however, individuals who did more than simply declare their New Year's resolutions, but actually wrote them out, were successful in achieving their objective 46 percent of the time – a ten-fold increase in achievement.

By delineating your objectives in writing you make a greater commitment to what you are attempting to achieve. Additionally, once you have reduced the committed objective to writing, you are providing yourself with a roadmap to success upon which to focus. To this end, there are two achievement tools used in Corporate America upon which you can rely: Balanced Scorecards and TQM

Balanced Scorecards

Widely used in corporate America, the balanced scorecard is a listing of objectives that the business feels it needs to accomplish to be successful. Generally, the objectives listed are items over which someone has complete control (e.g., making 100 cold calls per week) as opposed to items that we leave somewhat to chance (e.g., making $10,000 in sales each week from cold calling).

Certainly, with a balanced scorecard, you attempt to identify several objectives, each having a positive impact on success. That is, by completing an objective you increase the likelihood of being successful with respect to your designated goal.

Once you have a list of objectives, you should write them down. However, do not just write them out on a sheet of paper and then tuck them away where you will never see them again. Write down your overall goal and then detail the objectives you believe you need to complete to achieve this goal. Then you need to leave space for yourself to document the result.

Obviously, for purposes of this book, the goal is to improve your foundational networking – to get others to know you better, like you more and have greater trust in you. To this end, you have committed to this goal and you have written it down. Based on where you see deficiencies with respect to your foundational networking, you might conclude that you need to accomplish the following on a consistent basis to achieve this goal:

- **Acknowledgment Of Others (Presence)**: Each week, I will initiate and engage in a meaningful conversation with a perfect stranger.

- **Volunteerism (Altruism)**: Each month, I will commit to giving three hours to either charitable, community or school volunteering activities.

- **Role Recognition (Integrity)**: Each week, I will acknowledge the efforts of another person as being instrumental in helping me achieve my goals.

Then, periodically, you will document your results in writing on the particular objectives you have set for yourself. For example: During the week of May 24th, …

- **Acknowledgment Of Others (Presence)**: I introduced myself to Lewis Howes, founder of The Titan Zone and we had an interesting conversation about NCAA Division III college football.

- **Volunteerism (Altruism)**: I chaperoned a field trip for my son's class to the Air Force Museum.

- **Role Recognition (Integrity)**: I acknowledged Michael Diercks for his role in encouraging me to write this book.

In summary, your foundational networking balanced scorecard becomes an active worksheet of your goal to improve your foundational networking and the underlying objectives to make that happen.

Networking TQM

Total Quality Management (TQM) is a method by which management and employees become involved in the continuous improvement of a business.

Under TQM, a business focuses on all aspects of its organizational functions (i.e., marketing, finance, design, engineering, production, customer service, etc.) in an effort to identify opportunities for improvement ... Make the product less expensively ... Reduce job-related injuries ... Speeding up responses to customer complaints ... And on and on and on. In short, TQM is about making the business better, one aspect at a time.

In the 1950s, the Japanese asked W. Edward Deming, an American statistician and management theorist, to help them improve their war-torn economy. By implementing Deming's principles of TQM, Japan experienced dramatic economic growth. In the 1980s, when the United States began to see a reduction in its own world market share in relation to Japan, U.S. businesses rediscovered TQM.

As an extreme oversimplification, with TQM an organization will examine a process and document where failures or defects occur. For example, an insurance company might examine how it processes homeowners' policies. In so doing, it might determine that the third part of its triplicate policy form has a limited use. With this knowledge, the company would alter how it processes policies. This in turn would allow it to eliminate the third part as well as some duplicative processing efforts. The result would be cost savings and quicker policy processing.

While TQM has proven to be an effective process for improving a business' functioning, its application is not limited to corporate America.

TQM is also used in government, the military, education and in non-profit organizations. The principles of TQM can be applied to any process.

In fact, Ben Franklin, one of this country's founding fathers, applied a form of TQM as a means to improve interpersonal skills. Using Ben Franklin's innovation, Harry V. Roberts (University of Chicago) and Bernie F. Sergesketter (VP, AT&T) perfected the idea of personal TQM using modern concepts and tools in their book *Quality Is Personal: A Foundation for Total Quality Management*. Professor Wayne Baker (University of Michigan Business School) took this notion of personal TQM one step further in his book *Achieving Success Through Social Capital*, claiming that we can use the concepts of personal TQM "to manage the processes of building and using networks."

The notion behind Franklin's personal TQM, as perfected by Roberts and Sergesketter, is a checklist that tracks personal quality defects. For these purposes, a defect is simply a failure or lapse in your foundational networking. In other words, a defect is doing something you should not do or not doing something you should have done.

In *Achieving Success Through Social Capital*, Baker created a personal quality checklist for networking which he adapted from the work of Roberts and Sergesketter. On the left side of the page, vertically listed down the page are networking defects. Along the top of the page, horizontally listed across the page are units of time (perhaps days or weeks).

Following Baker's notion, you can develop your own expanded version of a "Foundational Networking" TQM Checklist. Some examples could include:

Presence

- I failed to say hello when someone made eye contact with me.
- I outwardly complained or commiserated about home or work.

Altruism

- I did not thank someone for his or her help.
- I failed to introduce an individual to my co-worker at the Chamber function.

Integrity

- I failed to listen to the opinion of someone.
- I blamed someone for a shortcoming at home or work.

Once you have your checklists populated with potential personal defects, the actual recording of data is relatively easy – simply make a check mark next to the listed shortcoming in the appropriate time slot. For example, if during week one of a particular month you failed to thank someone, you would put a check mark in the box where the vertical column of week one intersects with this particular failure row.

Be honest with yourself, as cheating hurts no one but you. Mark down even minor failures. After several weeks of recording and measuring, you will gain a sense as to what areas you need to improve.

Armed with this information about your shortcomings, you can take corrective action with respect to your behavior. For example, after several weeks you determine that you are having trouble getting around to thanking people. Knowing this and committing to correcting your behavior (or lack thereof), you decide to do something. In this instance, you might invest in some inexpensive "Thank You" cards to help make you more effective.

The ability to take corrective action regarding your behavior is not the main advantage of the Foundational Networking TQM. The main advantage is that it actually changes your behavior. That is because just knowing that you are tracking certain aspects of your behavior will have a positive effect on your performance. Again, whatever you measure, you will set about taking actions to improve.

Whether you employ a balanced scorecard, TQM or another method you have devised, you do not need to focus on all foundational attributes at once – even if each offers an area for improvement. You should select a handful (those three or four most vital to improving your foundational networking) and insert them into your monitoring process. Those you do not use today, you can reserve for future checklists.

The point to remember is that the underlying psychology of the Hawthorne Effect is powerful. You know you can improve your foundational networking. You have committed to doing this. Therefore, you ought to use tools of monitoring and measuring to see it through.

Envisioning Foundational Networking

> "Whatever you vividly imagine,
> ardently desire, sincerely believe,
> and enthusiastically act upon,
> must inevitably come to pass."
> — *Paul J. Meyer*

Another step – although not a final step as these should all be happening in concert – is simply seeing yourself become the person with whom you would like to associate. Again, foundational networking is about adopting the attitudes and developing the habits of those with whom you want to associate.

This is the notion of seeing the reality of what you expect to be. Essentially, you are projecting in your mind what it is you are striving to be. It is a bit of serious daydreaming.

This sort of projecting is routine for large multi-national companies. In his 1997 book, *The Living Company: Habits for Survival in a Turbulent Business Environment*, Arie de Geus indicates that studies show that successful long-term enterprises have at least some leaders and managers devoted to the useful question: "What will we do if such-and-such happens?"

This concept might seem to have more application to building a business than to improving foundational networking via developing presence, altruism and integrity. However, de Gues uses research from human psychology to demonstrate how companies emulate a particular aspect of human behavior: our ability to anticipate the future.

In *The Living Company*, de Gues discusses the work of David Ingvar, the head of the neurobiology department at the University of Lund in Sweden. Published in 1985, the results of Ingvar's research show that the human brain is constantly attempting to make sense of the future.

Apparently, every moment of your life, that supercomputer in your head instinctively creates action plans and programs for the future. Your subconscious works to anticipate the moment at hand, the next few minutes, the emerging hours, the days that follow, the coming weeks and years to come.

This activity occurs continually, throughout the day and as you sleep. It is important to note that these are not predictions and do not pretend to tell of what will happen. These are, rather, time paths into an anticipated future. For literally thousands of different situations, the brain sequences through a plethora of "If this happens, I will do that." Each path combines a future hypothetical condition of the environment with an option for action.

Not only does the brain make these time paths, it stores them. And because the brain stores them, you are able to visit these futures, remember your visits and learn from them. As de Gues states, "We have, in other words, a 'memory of the future' continually being formed and optimized in our imaginations and revisited time and time again."

One suggested function of future memory is to prepare you for action once one of the visited futures materializes. As such, your "memory of the future" serves your ability to build and maintain foundational networking activities.

By continually working through a variety of time paths associated with presence, altruism, and integrity, you will take on these characteristics. For example, you literally envision that when you walk into the room of strangers, you will cast a presence of self-confidence.

However, if the process of future memory is a subconscious activity, there is arguably little that you can do to enhance the effect. In short, continue to live and your memories of the future continue to build.

While it is true that you cannot directly control your subconscious thoughts, it makes sense that if you control your conscious thoughts, you cannot help but make an impact on the thoughts you have subconsciously.

This notion is behind much of what Paul J. Meyer has instilled in Leadership Management, Inc. (LMI), which provides programs and courses to aspiring business professionals and growing organizations related to all aspects of becoming more successful. Part of these programs is the use of affirmations.

An affirmation is simply, borrowing language from the LMI course material, "a positive declaration that describes what you want to be, what you want to have, or how you choose to live your life." For example, if the first thing in the morning you tell yourself in a firm and confident manner that "I will have a wonderful day," chances are that is exactly what the day will be. Or continually remind yourself through affirmation that:

- "I cast a commanding presence that attracts others to want to associate with me and engage themselves with what I am involved in."

- "I provide value to everyone with whom I associate ... I am a giver."

- "I have firmly rooted ethical values ... I am honest, reliable and trustworthy."

If you remind yourself of any (or all) of these thoughts on a consistent basis, they not only become part of the foreground of your conscious thinking, but also influence your subconscious thought patterns as well. As a result, these affirmations become reality, which in turn improves your foundational networking. Quoting Meyer, "Whatever you vividly imagine, ardently desire, sincerely believe and enthusiastically act upon, must inevitably come to pass."

In addition to affirmations, as you gear a large percentage of your thoughts to sight, a close ally of affirmation is visualization. Under LMI programs, participants learn that visualizing what they want or want to become is every bit as powerful as affirmations.

Following with one of the thoughts from above, not only would you say – *"I cast a commanding presence that attracts others to want to associate with me and engage themselves with what I am involved in."* – but you would envision yourself living this aspiration. For example, you might see yourself at a business networking event or social gathering where people congregate around you, drawn by your presence.

This visualization, if you visit it often consciously, will become part of your subconscious and play back into your future memory. Again, "Whatever we vividly imagine, ardently desire, sincerely believe and enthusiastically act upon, must inevitably come to pass." Soon, you will have a more commanding presence.

In addition to this, you can visualize yourself in most any situation.

- Using attributes from the section on presence, you can visualize yourself employing tasteful humor to endear yourself to people or exhibiting noble courage in the face of disappointment.

- Drawing from the section on altruism, you can work through different scenarios in which you are giving people compliments or providing much needed encouragement to someone.

- Working with material from the section on integrity, you can envision yourself better able to apologize for your faults and at the same time being more forgiving of those who have wronged you.

As you consciously think through these scenarios (or whatever aspects of improving your foundational networking you deem to be of importance), you cannot help but fuel your mind with material for subconscious thought. In so doing, your brain gets to work through and store time path after time path of how you will address situations in the future.

Then when one of the scenarios presents itself to you in the future, you immediately access the appropriate response or needed action, which has been carefully thought through time after time while you watch the game, sleep or shop. From this, people around you are impressed (and even amazed) at your ability to do just the right thing.

You know people like this. They always seemingly have the appropriate response or action for most any situation. They are usually calm and reflective. Why? It is for no other reason than that they have allowed, as well as empowered, their minds to work through the situation long before it occurs. There is no magic or secret here. They simply remember the future.

Foundational Networking In A Nutshell

> "With networking, skills and techniques
> are important. Attitudes and habits,
> however, are imperative."
> — *Frank Agin*

This book does not detail every attribute of the three underlying aspects of foundational networking. The broad topics contained in *Foundational Networking* entail many things – more than anyone could reasonably put in a 225-page book.

What this book does, however, is exactly what I said on the opening line: Change the way you think about networking. You now know that networking success is not about you mastering skills and techniques. While those are important, they are hardly imperative.

What is imperative is that people know you, like you and trust you. The process of building the know, like and trust within your network entails maintaining and improving your presence, exhibiting and enhancing your altruism and bolstering your integrity.

That is foundational networking. It is about being the best possible person you can be. It is about adopting the attitudes and habits that you admire in other people with whom you want to associate – become the person you want to be with.

Therefore, when you have that insightful moment and encounter an attribute of presence, altruism or integrity that you did not read about in this book, do not despair. Rather, embrace your discovery and add it to your own personal practices of foundational networking. In so doing, those you know and come to know will know you better, like you more and trust you further.

Through foundational networking, you should aspire to become the person with whom you want to associate.

Summary Notes
For Foundational Networking

Effective professional networking is not a function of strong interpersonal skills and techniques. It is, however, dependent on a solid regimen of foundational networking.

Foundational Networking is the process of building know, like and trust in your relationships, which is done whenever you focus on the attitudes and habits that serve to:

- Improve your *Presence*
- Enhance Your *Altruism*
- Bolster your *Integrity*

Presence

Presence is the impression you leave on others, whether through in-person contact or communication via written form, telephone or e-mail.

Sense of Humor: When used appropriately, humor will make people more comfortable around you.

High Expectations: Always look for more in your life – both personally and professionally. Be the person working toward and expecting to achieve something wonderful. Others want to associate with that potential.

Contagiously Energetic: To energize others, and thereby make yourself known to them and get them to like and trust you, give them a vision and trust them to contribute and become involved in what you are doing.

Actively Involved: You should always set an example of action, effort, and achievement. Others are drawn to the benefits this could mean for them.

Situational Acceptance: You should always want more, but accept the circumstances and situation that life has given you. This will make others more comfortable in associating with you.

Courageous Determination: You naturally draw people towards you when you forge ahead despite a disappointing setback. Never give up.

Authentic Affection: Work to find good qualities in people you meet and adopt the attitude of wanting to like them. People want to be liked and want to associate with those who like them.

Acknowledgement Of Others: Take an interest in others and work to make them feel comfortable around you. People are naturally attracted to those who make them feel comfortable.

Sportsmanship: When you exhibit elements of good sportsmanship, you set a wonderful example that elevates your presence in others' eyes. People then want to associate with you whether or not things are going well.

Authenticity: Always project on the outside a true reflection of your inside self. This will give those with whom you associate a consistent view of who you are and it will give them a better sense of trusting you.

Genuine Happiness: People want to associate with happy people. Think about things that make you happy and keep a smile on your face. It will change your day, as a cheerful disposition will draw others to you.

Unpretentious: Take pride in who you are and what you do, but be humble enough to recognize that everyone adds value to the world. People want to associate with those who have an appreciation of them.

Personal Accountability: All that you are and all that you are not is simply a function of your achievements and failures. Do not be afraid to acknowledge that. This candor will draw others to you.

Altruism

Altruism is the habit of giving to the world around you. Eventually what you inject into your network – opportunities, information, support, energy and additional contacts – comes back to you, mainly in the form of people wanting to associate with you.

Compassion: Attempt to identify with others' challenges ... their stresses, insecurities, struggles, regrets, and disappointments. This exercise will help you develop a heightened sense of how you can contribute to the lives of others.

Encouragement: There is tremendous value in providing someone with moral support in times of trouble, even if that is all you can do.

Smiles: When you smile, you cause others to smile with you. When they smile, they gain an uplifting feeling.

Volunteerism: Giving your time and talents to charitable organizations, civic associations and local schools offers myriad opportunities to fortify and add to your network.

Compliments: Offering compliments to others costs you nothing, but it serves to improve their self-esteem as well as your stature in their eyes.

Appreciation: Take every opportunity to say "thank you" whether via spoken word, written note or special action, such as sending a gift. This will give others the sense of feeling appreciated.

Attention: When you really listen to someone – comprehending what is being said, seeking clarification and being eager to learn more – you give validation to them.

Gracious Receipt: Others want to give you gifts or assistance, especially if you have given to them. To have strong relationships, you must learn to open yourself to the contributions of others and graciously accept them, thereby giving them the joy of helping you.

Thoughtfulness: Focus on ways in which you can be considerate of others' feelings and find ways you can have a positive impact on their lives in any way, big or small.

True Bigheartedness: There is no rhyme or reason as to when or how much your generosity will return to you. The triumphs of others are your gains, too, and their struggles are your struggles, so you should always be ready to lend a helping hand, even if you might not receive anything in return.

Personal Introductions: Altruism is not limited by your personal wealth, professional experience or influence. Bringing people together from different segments of your life can be invaluable to others.

Unsolicited Generosity: Altruism is not so much what you give but the spirit that moves you to give, or your motivation for giving. You maximize the amount of joy you share when others do not know it is coming.

Integrity

Integrity involves the habits and attitudes that allow others to feel comfortable interacting with you.

Consistent Comfort: How you make others feel through your interactions with them has a direct relationship with the level of integrity that they determine you have. You should endeavor to continually make others feel comfortable and at ease in associating with you.

Trusting Nature: If you want others to trust you, you need to trust them first. People associate with (and trust) those who trust them.

Role Recognition: People are energized by and appreciative of you when you openly share the credit associated with achievement (whether large or small) with those around you.

Reliability: The greatest compliment is being known as reliable because it means that others feel that they can turn to you (or refer others to you) and count on the results. Always do what you say you will do.

Honesty: Even if no one else knows, choose the path of sincerity, truthfulness, and integrity versus one of disingenuousness, deceit, and treachery. By doing so, you will be further ahead in the end.

Acts Of Contrition: When you do wrong – whether intentional or not – you should never be too proud to say, "I'm sorry." You will diminish or disarm anger others may feel toward you and bolster your character in others' eyes at the same time.

Personal Responsibility: Be cautious in how and when you blame others for occasional misfortunes you encounter. Carefully examine your contribution to the mishap first. This provides you an opportunity for growth and allows you to preserve relationships in the process.

Forgiveness: Forgiving others allows you to divert energy to more productive and creative endeavors and adds to your own health and happiness as well as gives others comfort in associating with you.

Open Mindedness: Share your opinions responsibly, but remember they are not definitive facts. As such, remember that others are entitled to their own opinions. If you meet someone with a differing opinion on one subject, agree to disagree and work to find common ground on another subject. By doing so, others will find comfort in associating with you.

Tactfulness: Develop the habit of reflecting on situations before you take action. It does not matter so much what you do or say but how you do or say it. Using tact requires that you exhibit consideration, kindness, and reason.

Appropriate Motivation: Avoid manipulation, and make sure your objectives are truly in everyone's best interest. Motivation is nothing more than finding objectives that are good for both others and you and then encouraging others to take the actions that will help achieve those objectives.

Conscientious Influence: Do not use your position of power to unfairly coerce someone to do something you want them to do. You will gain respect, admiration, and the trust of others by using your position responsibly.

Endnotes

Presence

- *Beliefs Can Influence Attitudes*, Nell Mohney, Abingdon Press

- *The Hidden Power of Social Networks*: *Understanding How Work Really Gets Done in Organizations*, Rob Cross and Andrew Parker, Harvard Business School Publishing Corporation

- *Eleven Seconds: A Story of Tragedy, Courage & Triumph*, Travis Roy and E.M. Swift, Warner Books

- *The 17 Essential Qualities Of A Teamplayer*, John C. Maxwell, Thomas Nelson Publishing

- *Blink*, Malcolm Gladwell, Little, Brown and Company, Time Warner Book Group

- *QBQ: The Question Behind The Question – What To Really Ask Yourself To Eliminate Blame*, Complaining and Procrastination, John G. Miller, G.P. Putnam's Sons (Penguin Group (USA))

Altruism

- *People Power: 12 Power Principles to Enrich Your Business, Career & Personal Networks*, Donna Fisher, Bard & Stephen Publishers

- *Rambam's Ladder*, Julie Salamon, Workman Publishing Company

- *Wrestlers Share Magical Moment*, Craig Sesker, *Omaha World-Herald*, December 17, 2003

- *The Success Journey*, John C. Maxwell, Thomas Nelson Publishing

- *Bringing Out The Best In People*, Alan Loy McGinnis, Augsburg Fortress Publishing

- *Ten Things I Learned From Bill Porter*, Shelly Brady, New World Library

- *Facial Expressions Are Contagious*, *Journal of Psychophysiology*, 1995, Lars-Olov Lundquist & Ulf Dimberg

- *Dare To Connect*, Susan Jeffers, Ballantine Books

- *Nonstop Networking*, Andrea Nierenberg, Capital Books

- *Winning With People*, John C. Maxwell, Thomas Nelson Publishing

- *Winning Without Intimidation*, Bob Burg, Samark Publishing

Integrity

- *Integrity Outweighs Winning For High-School Golf Star*, Bob Hunter, The Columbus Dispatch, October 19, 2005

- *Left To Tell: Discovering God Amidst the Rwandan Holocaust*, Immaculee Ilibagiza, Hay House

Foundational Networking Improvement

- *Selling The Invisible*, Harry Beckwith, Warner Books

- *Quality Is Personal: A Foundation for Total Quality Management*, Harry V. Roberts and Bernie F. Sergesketter, The Free Press

- *Achieving Success Through Social Capital*, Wayne Baker, Jossey-Bass

Envisioning Foundational Networking

- *The Living Company: Habits for Survival in a Turbulent Business Environment*, Arie de Geus, Harvard Business School Publishing

- Paul J. Meyer, Leadership Management Inc.

Are You Looking For More?

If you are interested in being further empowered and inspired by foundational networking or networking in general, then:

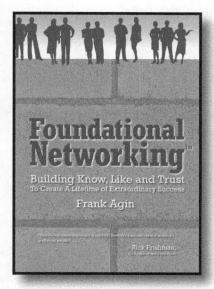

Visit
www.foundationalnetworking.com… to read more insights on foundational networking or to share your own.

Visit
www.amspirit.com… to learn about the AmSpirit Business Connections program or to obtain information on franchise opportunities.

Am*Spirit*™
BUSINESS *CONNECTIONS*

Contact Frank Agin at
frankagin@amspirit.com …
to discuss having him speak to
or conduct training and facilitation
within your company or organization

Frank Agin Biography

Frank Agin is the founder and president of AmSpirit Business Connections, an organization that empowers entrepreneurs, sales representatives and professionals to become more successful through the practice of developing stronger business relationships. In addition to *Foundational Networking*, Frank has written dozens of articles and delivered hundreds of programs on achieving greater success through stronger professional relationships. *Foundational Networking* is an accumulation of his life experiences, observations and investigation as it relates to professional relationships. He is a graduate of Beloit College and has a law degree and MBA from the Ohio State University. He lives near Columbus, Ohio with his wife and three children.

9 780982 333211